THE PASTORAL IDEA

THE PASTORAL IDEA

*Lectures on Pastoral Theology delivered at
King's College, London, during the
Lent Term,* 1905

BY

JAMES THEODORE INSKIP, M.A.

VICAR OF LEYTON

WITH A PREFACE BY

THE RIGHT REVEREND
THE LORD BISHOP OF ST. ALBANS

London

MACMILLAN AND CO., Limited

NEW YORK : THE MACMILLAN COMPANY

1905

GLASGOW: PRINTED AT THE UNIVERSITY PRESS
BY ROBERT MACLEHOSE AND CO. LTD.

TO MY FATHER
IN GRATITUDE FOR HIS
EXAMPLE AND
TEACHING

PREFACE.

I HAVE read with great interest and desire to commend to the public this little volume of lectures on Pastoral Theology, delivered by a leading incumbent of London-over-the-Border in my diocese, to Theological students of King's College during the past spring.

Pastoral Theology has a freshness for every generation, for the conditions of life and work vary so greatly that the man who simply uses old methods and fails to understand the generation in which he lives will fail to touch many who are capable of being won and converted into active workers for the Master.

Mr. Inskip's experience in South London, in Cornwall, and in London-over-the-Border has fitted him for the task which was laid upon him by the Council of King's College, and I am persuaded that clergy as well as Theological students will do well to read his counsels and to lay them to heart.

EDGAR ALBAN :

HIGHAMS, WOODFORD GREEN,
August 8, 1905.

PREFATORY NOTE.

THE title-page of this volume shews that the book does not pretend to be a complete manual of the duties of a clergyman. A course of ten lectures to candidates for Holy Orders allows only of setting before one's hearers some thoughts suggested by a few years' parochial experience. And the thoughts have been put into shape amidst the pressure of work in an arduous and rapidly growing parish.

Many of John Strype's works were sent forth to the world from the vicarage at Leyton, where he was incumbent from 1669 to 1737. His latest successor is not only devoid of Strype's learning, but is denied the comparative leisure which was the lot of the vicar when Leyton was a country village near London with a church standing in the park.

My thanks are due to the Principal of King's College and to the members of the staff of the Theological Faculty for their kindness during my year of office as Special

Lecturer, as also to the members of the Faculty for the attentive hearing which they gave to the lectures. I must also thank the Bishop of St. Albans for reading the proof-sheets and contributing the Preface. Several friends, in particular the Rev. R. Cobden Earle, have kindly allowed me to print accounts of incidents, which would otherwise have been of a confidential character. My own colleagues, past and present, have laid me under an obligation in this respect, and the Rev. Richard Elliott has given me useful help in the preparation of the first lecture.

The ideals in the lectures may not be lofty enough for the requirements of some earnest souls, but, such as they are, I am conscious of falling far short of them in my own work. Anything which is good in them I owe under God to the teaching and influence of others, not least my former Principal, the Bishop of Durham; while I cannot be too thankful for the opportunity of beginning work under the Rev. W. H. Stone, now Vicar of St. Mary's, Kilburn, a master in every branch of parochial ministration.

J. T. INSKIP.

THE VICARAGE, LEYTON, E.,
  16th August 1905.

CONTENTS.

I.

THE IDEA OF THE PASTORATE.

In the old days an impression prevailed that almost anyone was good enough to be a clergyman. Heresies die hard, and this impression may still linger in certain quarters of society, but it no longer has the smallest basis in fact. This is easily proved. The demand for clergymen is greater than ever it was, the call for more men is heard loudly on all sides; yet in these days of overcrowded professions and severe competition for a livelihood the number of accepted candidates for Holy Orders declines. There is no lack of aspirants, but a certain standard of intellectual attainment and a certain period of preparation, if not of training, are demanded. And the standard is maintained. That this is true is known to many who have aspired in vain to enter the gate which gives access to the

Ministry. All this bespeaks a more charitable view of the calibre expected in a clergyman by the man of the world. It also bespeaks a higher view of the ministerial office and a more serious estimate of the difficulty of its task—to lead men to believe not only in a Deity, but in God, and to desire fellowship with Him through Jesus Christ whom He has sent. Never was the task more difficult than in this materialistic age, when belief in the unseen, the spiritual, the divine, the eternal is so faltering, unless as exhibited in the pretensions of such crazes as spiritualism, theosophy or Christian science.

The difficulty of the calling has not deterred you from readiness to accept it, but your recognition of the nature of the task before you leads you to hear not only what men of profound learning can unfold to you out of the treasury of their own knowledge, but also what one pretending to nothing but practical experience can tell you of the work of the Ministry to-day. Learning and scholarship will help to reveal to you the meaning of the word Theology, but the outcome of practical experience may help you to understand the Pastoral idea. And it is as Lecturer in Pastoral Theology that I appear before you. In these Lectures I do not propose to enter in detail into any questions of scholarship. For guidance there you will look to other quarters. My concern is with the work out in the world which you will soon be called to take up. And though there is nothing like your own personal experience for giving an insight into the best means of fulfilling pastoral obligations, yet the result of the experience of a brother may aid you both in laying down the lines on which you will first proceed, and in avoiding mistakes which mere theory, however good, might not keep you from committing. And in addressing you I have one advantage which might not obtain with a similar audience else-where—most of you have seen something from within of the work which I shall describe, and you will therefore be able to follow more sympathetically the outlines which I wish to draw.

What is the meaning of the term Pastoral Theology? Is it not Applied Theology?—the application of what we know of God to the needs of man?

Such knowledge and such application of it are not confined to any one order of men. The days have long since passed when priests alone were authorized to know. The layman may attain as profound a knowledge of God as may the clergyman. And the layman may—one would like to say must—share in applying that knowledge to human needs. Yet the knowledge of God and its application to men are the special functions of the Christian Ministry. "We will give ourselves continually to prayer and to the ministry of the word" (Acts vi. 4). In speaking of the 'special functions' of the clergy, one is reminded that the word 'special' is a modern justification for the continuance of the office of a clergyman. Never was its existence more justified than to-day, when specialization is the keynote of study and of work, and is carried to an almost extreme degree.

The Ministers of Christ are to be specialists in two departments—as a modern writer[1] reminds us—(1) the knowledge of God, and (2) the knowledge of men.

Man's nature and character are to be their particular interest and study. Man as presented in the Bible, so true a mirror of what manner of men we are, is to be familiar to them. And they are to understand man as seen in the world to-day. This special knowledge will be useful, but not enough by itself. It may help to make a good critic, a

[1] *The Clerical Life* (Hodder & Stoughton, 1898), pages 62, 64.

clever cynic or a smart novelist, or even a
man of the world in a good sense. But it will
never bring men to God. It is not enough
to diagnose a complaint without knowing or
applying a remedy. So while we remember
the saying,

"Humani nihil a me alienum puto,"

we shall err if we limit our observation and
study to the world. The newspaper, the
review and the magazine must not be our
only or even our chief resort. Something
more is required.

The Ministers of Christ must also be
specialists in the knowledge of God. They
must know God ; they must know about God.
They must have 'tasted of the heavenly gift,
and have been made partakers of the Holy
Ghost, and have tasted the good word of
God, and the powers of the world to come'
(Hebrews vi. 4, 5). They must breathe the
air of heaven, and they must be animated by
another spirit, which leads them to follow
God fully. They must be in the world, but
not of it. They must be men of God. Without the knowledge of God a clergyman will
belie his profession, will discredit his calling,
and will damage the souls of others.

At the same time, the specialist in the knowledge of God will not be effective as a clergyman unless he knows something of men. It is his duty to communicate what he knows of God to others, to interpret what is clear to himself but hidden from them, to deliver God's message in a language understanded of the people. Without some knowledge of men his force and influence will be seriously crippled and impaired,

Theories may be very good on paper, but they are apt to break down in practice. Pastoral Theology, however, points the way to apply in the world what we have learned in the schools.

The word Pastoral carries us in thought to the country. And as most of us will be working in large towns, it is well that it does so. For the country seems to speak of what is good and pure, fresh and elevating, restful to the eye, and healthy or mind and body. There we see nature, and there nature tells of God. With some truth it is said that " man made the town, but God made the country." The life of our modern great towns does, alas ! go far to shut out God. They savour so much of the merely human, of so-called civilization, and that often on its sordid side. And there is little in what

men see round them there to lift their thoughts
to God.   Humanitarians (not to speak of
Christians) feel that things have gone too far.
The villages have swarmed into our towns, and
masses of people are herded together under
conditions which make the work of the Church
increasingly difficult.   So to-day the aim of
many is to bring a suggestion of country into
the town—to lay out parks and open spaces, to
plant trees, to encourage the growth of flowers,
to let in fresh air in abundance.   And with this
goes the movement to take the town down to
the country—to transfer factories and railway
works, to erect garden cities, to board out in
the villages our waifs and strays, and to take
the children of our crowded parishes for an
annual fortnight amongst our fields and dales.

Our work for God in great cities seems to
have caught the inspiration of country life.
Do we not in miles of squalid streets in
London exercise *pastoral* visitation ? Have
we not our *Rural* Deaneries, even in Spitalfields and Bethnal Green ? And in Stepney
or the Borough shepherding work has to be
done, for the thousands of souls massed there
are sheep of Christ's flock whom His shepherds
are sent to seek and to save.

The Pastoral idea comes from the Bible, and

is commended to us by our Lord Himself. It
is indeed not limited to the Bible. Classical
literature regards the shepherding of the people
as being a special function of their rulers.
Homer, for instance, calls Agamemnon ποιμένα
λαῶν. When we turn to the books of the Old
Testament we find frequent reference to the
idea. Israel is at times spoken of as sheep
without a shepherd. Jeremiah and Ezekiel
describe the kings and rulers of Judah as the
pastors of the people, and use terms of
denunciation regarding their neglect which
would require very little modernizing to apply
to neglect of spiritual work to-day. But the
highest conception is given by David—" The
Lord is my Shepherd" (Psalm xxiii. 1).
How far the utterances of the Psalmist
were Messianic it is needless for us to discuss. They at least prepare the way for the
use of the figure by our Lord Himself. St.
John delights to quote our Lord's use of the
title ; " I am the Good Shepherd : the Good
Shepherd giveth His life for the sheep " (St.
John x. 11). " I am the Good Shepherd, and
know My sheep, and am known of Mine"
(x. 14). We must avoid titles for, or views
of, the ministerial office which are not of our
Lord's own choice or do not naturally grow out

of His teaching as developed and interpreted by the Apostles. But this title, as well as the office and its functions, we derive from our Lord Himself. Of the titles which He ascribed to Himself, none can more appropriately describe the ministerial office than that of Shepherd, for its imagery was borrowed by our Lord when committing the care of His people to St. Peter. This description of the office St. Paul quotes : " He gave some . . . Pastors and Teachers " (Ephesians iv. 11). And our own Church keeps this conception of the Ministry before her sons, appointing for Epistle and Gospel at the Ordering of Priests those passages in which the thought occurs, and pursuing the same line in the exposition of the Priest's office which follows.

Let us study then our Lord's conception of Himself and of His ministers as Shepherds or Pastors. Let us observe His own character in that capacity : His fulfilment of the office : the words and acts which it involved: His methods in dealing with the flock or with individual sheep : His plans for us : the teaching which we are to make our own and to pass on to others. Note the idea of feeding and tending the flock : His thought, care and attention in their service : His readiness to sacrifice His own life : His desire to know the sheep and to be known by them.

The term does not include the whole idea of the Christian Ministry. No single word could do so. The illustration was not complete—not even for His servants, still less for our Lord. But He used it of Himself. And we may well be proud to accept the designation.

No apology is needed for taking the idea as the keynote of my addresses to you, and as the framework of their structure. I hope to keep near to the development of the idea found in Scripture, yet to bear in mind modern needs. For though our principles remain unchanged, we must adapt our system, our methods, our language, ourselves to the age in which we live.

It may be urged that the word 'Pastor' has been somewhat spoilt by its use as an official, even a professional, title by several Christian denominations, and that its adoption savours to some minds of cant. And it is perhaps true that those who have adopted the term have not always exhibited that masculinity which we should wish to mark our character. We must, however, if necessary rescue the word. At any rate we must not disdain a title so dear to our Lord.

Nor need we be frightened at the readiness

of many to associate with the very idea of pastoral care a gentleness and a tenderness which seem to some minds effeminate and weak. Christianity itself is assailed on this very point. Hear the late Samuel Laing in his *Problems of the Future* (ch. viii.) : " The Christian ideal, to a great extent, ignored courage, hardihood, self-reliance, foresight, providence and all the sterner and harder qualities that make the man, for the softer and more feminine virtues of love, patience and resignation." Those very virtues are the glory of the Christian character. And the agnostic critic does not seem to realize that perfection of character lies partly in the balance of the qualities of hardiness and gentleness.

One of Bishop Lightfoot's published sermons deals with the career of Bernard Gilpin, the 'Apostle of the North,' in the sixteenth century. In appraising Gilpin's character the Bishop remarks: "Unworldliness and courage, when developed in a very high degree, are commonly associated with some weakness or defect of character in the opposite direction. . . . The courageous man is hard, exacting, unsympathetic. Bernard Gilpin's character is open to no such charges. We are especially struck with the even balance

of his character. No one good quality is
developed at the expense of the other. He
is bold and fearless, and yet tender and loving" (*Leaders of the Northern Church*, p. 133).
The little child may sing, "Jesus, Tender
Shepherd, hear me," without making the Great
Shepherd of souls any the less suited for the
devotion of the strong man. It is no detrac-
tion from the character of our Blessed Lord
that He should be such. Isaiah's words recur
to us, "He shall feed His flock like a shepherd, He shall gather the lambs with His
arm, and carry them in His bosom" (xl. 11).
Of the same God of whom David could sing,
"He teacheth my hands to war; so that a
bow of steel is broken by mine arms," he
could the next moment add, "Thy gentleness
hath made me great" (2 Samuel xxii. 36).

That gentleness we not only want to draw
upon in our own ministry, but on it we rely
for our actual preservation. By it we are
assured that our Lord will look in mercy and
pity on our poor efforts to serve Him. "He
remembereth that we are dust" (Psalm ciii.
14); "If thou, Lord, wilt be extreme to
mark what is done amiss: O Lord, who
may abide it?" (Psalm cxxx. 3, Pr. Bk.
Version).

Even men of the world will appreciate this tenderness. The agnostic—in spite of Samuel Laing—will soon note its absence, or will actually be moved by its presence. In a parish where I formerly worked there lived an old cooper. He was a rough-looking man, and lived in his latter years much as he had done in his working days—amidst his tools in his actual shop. He was thoughtful, but a pronounced agnostic. Beneath the gruff exterior breathed the gentlest of spirits, unaffected by the discomfort of his lonely life or by the theft of half his savings in an unbelieving world. On the Christian faith, alas! his mind was made up, and the arguments of the clergy did not move him. But one day the district visitor left with him a framed picture of the Good Shepherd. The old man's heart was touched, and the picture found a prominent place in his home. When I left the parish the dear old cooper had not confessed return to God, but the appeal of the Good Shepherd went home, and I can only trust that when a few months ago he passed away he had returned to the Shepherd and Bishop of his soul.

No—we need not be ashamed of the tenderness of the Good Shepherd. Men want tending—they want tenderness, and many a hard heart is melted by receiving it. Sentiment need not become sentimentality, and emotion need not turn to effeminacy. We must not be ashamed of shewing feeling. There is nothing unmanly in this. In marking the perfect Man, and following His example, we cannot go far wrong.

In other ways we want to reflect in our own minds the mind which was in Christ Jesus. We must therefore try to gain some insight into the Chief Shepherd's purpose and plan. We do not know the whole mind of our Master, but we know enough. Our blessed Lord's purpose was to gather out of the world—from every nation, age and clime —a people for Himself. On earth they were to form a society. This was not to continue here for ever, but only until the purpose of the Founder could be fully realized—the making His Name known to every nation. " This Gospel of the Kingdom shall be preached in all the world for a witness unto all nations: and then shall the end come" (St. Matthew xxiv. 14). A definite term of work is assigned to the Church. As with the individual man, so with the Church, her earthly life is limited, and a certain work has to be accomplished in her lifetime. Too often the individual man forgets this, too often the Church at large forgets it as well. 'The end' means a conclusion not to everything, but to the present order, and the ushering in of a new regime. This is connected with the Second Coming of our Lord, and whatever view we take of the details of His Coming we shall all agree on the importance of keeping the Advent of our Glorified Lord before our minds as an article of faith. We must make it more than that—there must be a looking for, and a looking forward to His glorious appearing. One fears that a want of this is a grave defect in the Christian Church to-day. I may be mistaken: I trust that my impression is incorrect. But it is certain that a keen expectation of our Lord's Second Coming will quicken the pace at which we do the work which our Lord wishes to be done—in certain other work the pace of the Christian Church is too rapid already. The spirit of expectation will also keep before us the particular aim which ought to mark our parochial work.

We are too apt—especially in large parishes —to do a certain amount of work and to fulfil a certain round of duties, without looking upon each day's toil as an integral part of our own ministry, and as a portion of the great work of the Church as a whole. During our term of service we are to build a certain section of the great spiritual Temple, and a few bricks must be laid every day. We are to bring a certain number of sheep into the great Flock and to tend them when they are there; every day we must try to bring in some more and to tend the sheep which are already committed to our care.

All must be done in the expectation of our Lord's Second Coming. Our daily work must be subscribed, " I look for the resurrection of the dead, and the life of the world to come." Our Lord's own prayer was : " Father, I will that they also, whom Thou hast given Me, be with Me where I am ; that they may behold My glory, which Thou hast given Me " (St. John xvi. 24).

If this spirit be missing in our own case, we can only receive it from our Lord Himself. By faith we are in union with Christ—one with Him, and He one with us. But this union must not only exist—we know it exists ; it must also be realized. Meditation, study, prayer and the Holy Communion will help to bring it home to us. So will our minds reflect more the mind of Christ.

All this will need time and care.   There must be a daily yielding and submission of our minds to the influence of the mind of Christ.   We must come to Him with open mind and open heart, ready to receive the impression which He will make.   So will our characters be gradually formed more after the likeness of Christ.

We can readily understand the reason why our Lord drew and kept His disciples so closely round Himself during the years of His Ministry.   Generally speaking they were with Him nearly all the time, and the 'training of the Twelve' occupied much of His thought and care.   There were also special occasions of retirement from the world for converse with Himself.   The Forty Days between the Resurrection and Ascension gave one such opportunity, and the first commission to the Apostles was given with words suggestive of a similar idea: "He ordained twelve, that they should be with Him, and that He might send them forth to preach" (St. Mark iii. 14).

It may seem unnecessary to speak at any length of the importance of this.   Yet the subject must not be passed by.   Men who hope to take Holy Orders are sometimes

B

tempted to cut the period of preparation short, or, if the wise regulations of the Episcopate prevent this, to wish to cut it short. And this temptation appeals especially to those who have begun life in some other career, and who naturally therefore desire the period of transition to be as short as possible. But as years go by the difficulties of the work of the Ministry wear a more serious aspect. Some of us who have been ordained can remember how even in the happy days of life at our Theological College we longed for the time when we should be in harness. Did we realize the difficulty of meeting the great responsibilities of ministerial life?

Some frank words written by the Principal of Salisbury Theological College on the subject of the late Father Dolling's preparation for the ministry may illustrate this danger: "I think he must have regarded his time spent here as an irritating interruption or postponement of the life's work awaiting him. With all his wonderful powers in other directions, his weak point lay in a thinly disguised contempt for formal study. For myself, I have no doubt that but for this failure he would have filled a still greater place in the history of the Church of this land" (Prebendary Whitefoord in *Life of Father Dolling*, p. 43).

No time granted to us for preparation is too long. The more one sees into the mind of Christ, the more difficult it appears to present or to represent that mind to the world, or even to the Church, and one feels increasingly the need of dwelling with the King for His work both in preparing for and after entering the work of the Ministry.

The 'being with' our Lord, the 'sitting at the feet of Jesus' must ever go on. There is always more to be learnt. After taking the yoke of Christ upon us, we are to learn of Him. The grave of John Richard Green at Mentone bears the inscription, "He died learning." So should die the Minister of Christ. And if he is to die learning, he must live learning. The activities of parochial life and the exigencies of its demands must not take us away from Christ. There must be daily prayer, study of God's Word and meditation, if our work is to be more than a perfunctory round of duties, or the carrying on of a spiritual business. The time for this will best be early in the day. You will probably attend Morning Prayer in your parish church before breakfast; afterwards

will come school work, or—if unhappily
there are no day-schools connected with the
church—parishioners will call on various quests,
and letters will demand attention, and after that
the preparation of sermons will occupy some
hours. So you will only get a quiet time with
God before your early service. This may mean
early rising, which will be difficult for many.

In speaking of difficulty here I have no
sympathy with those who through habits of
laziness find early rising a weariness of the
flesh. But I think rather of those who "so
late take rest, and eat the bread of careful-
ness" (Psalm cxxvii. 2, Pr. Bk. Version), and
who are physically scarcely able to rise at an
early hour. Some such do rise early, curtail-
ing proper hours of sleep. The late Archbishop Benson used to retire to rest very late
—one of his chaplains states in the Biography
of the Archbishop that he often worked on
until one or two in the morning. For many
years he never slept for more than "five
hours and ten minutes" in any night, and he
would—even when forbidden to work before
breakfast—rise about seven, giving much time
to reading the Bible. In his earlier days he
rose at half-past five, and spent an hour before
breakfast over the Greek Testament or at a

book on the Revelation (*Life*, vol. i. ch. xvii.). In view of such an example we need not complain of being hard pressed, if our rest is somewhat curtailed at both ends.

The late hours which are kept by dwellers in large towns, and especially by inhabitants of London, may make it impossible for us to retire to rest early. We may be burdened with parochial organization, or church accounts— and whatever share may be taken by laymen, some must fall on the clergy. We may be engrossed in the prosecution of some special branch of study, or in writing a book—likely perhaps to benefit the writer more than the reader, and only late at night can we find a quiet hour. Perhaps the task of building a new church or of raising large funds presses heavily upon us. Late hours may seem un- avoidable, but they may rob us of our quiet time with God twice every day. We are so late in retiring that the opportunity for even- ing devotions has passed away, and we rise so late the next morning that parochial duties press on us the moment that we come down- stairs. We cannot, however, pass over our private devotions, and though it may be questioned whether we are obliged to say the office of Morning and Evening Prayer, a little effort will probably enable us to find time for our Church service as well.

Very wise on spiritual grounds as well as on physical was the advice which Bishop Chavasse used to give at Oxford—to form a habit of retiring to rest in good time. We may almost say that early retiring and early rising are generally necessary to spiritual health. A friend of my own was asked by his Bishop at the time of his ordination whether he were an early riser. The question appeared to shew great insight on the part of the Bishop, because early rising was not one of his many virtues. For a moment my friend was tempted to suppose that he did possess the faculty in question, but candour overcame self-deception, and he replied that he was not an early riser. " Neither am I," replied the Bishop. But the question and its importance have never faded from my friend's memory. You will probably soon find out the importance of what I urge, if you do not know it already, for the layman needs his morning watch with God. Failure as well as faithfulness in this respect will endorse the estimate of its value

In such ways we must seek to know our Blessed Lord more fully, and to know more about Him, His purposes, His plans. We shall thus be better enabled to carry on His work, moved by His Spirit. The Lord will then send us forth to teach and—if not to cast out devils—to prove of corresponding blessing, to banish sin and to bring in righteousness. A sense of mission from Himself will keep us right in our view of the ministerial office. We are to enter it not to draw all we can out of life or out of the world, but to be and to do all in our power for the world. The man who has little in common with God naturally turns to the world to satisfy himself; he therefore draws from the world. But it is our part to give to the world some share of that grace which we have drawn from the Living God in private communion and in the use of the means of grace. We may not therefore even unconsciously and unintentionally look chiefly at the emoluments or the importance of the positions which we occupy or hope to occupy. We may not get all we can out of our parishes in the way of personal advantage. One hears certain parishes spoken of as 'stepping-stones.' The phrase is most objectionable. The unfortunate parishioners are to be used as a lever to elevate their clergyman to a higher or more remunerative ecclesiastical position. But the question at the end of life will be not how far we have raised ourselves, but how far we have raised our people. And the true pastor will be continually thinking of the impression which he can make upon his people, an impression not of himself, but of Christ. If we are thinking of ourselves, our income, our position, even our success, our attention will be diverted from Christ to ourselves. The centre of our work will then be self instead of the people. We shall become more and more selfish. But if parish and people come nearest to our hearts, thoughts of personal ease and comfort will disappear. This is the explanation of what the Bishop of St. Albans says in a recent letter to his diocese asking help for the Diocesan Poor Benefices Fund: "I admire the patience with which the hardships of poverty are borne in many a gentle home where the struggle of life is no bar to the tenderness and sympathy that goes out to the sick and needy in the parish entrusted to the incumbent's charge." The need of having some grace to bestow, to diffuse, to distribute, will drive us afresh to the Lord. We cannot give, unless we first receive.

The sense of mission will come home to

us again and again. "Ye have not chosen Me, but I have chosen you, and ordained you, that ye should go and bring forth fruit, and that your fruit should remain" (St. John xv. 16). These words were the text of the sermon at my ordination, and it is no disparagement to the preacher to say that, though every word of his own has long since been forgotten, his text has never faded from my memory and has often proved of comfort and strength. What better purpose could a sermon serve ?

This sense of mission is not dependent upon our knowledge of the history of the Christian Ministry. Into a critical examination of its foundation and constitution it is needless here to enter. Enough for us that there is such a Ministry. The Preface to the Ordinal says: "It is evident unto all men diligently reading the Holy Scripture and ancient authors, that from the Apostles' time there have been these Orders of Ministers in Christ's Church; Bishops, Priests, and Deacons." We may not follow these words to the very letter, or we may go with them heart and soul. We may go to the extremes of Hatch on the one hand or of Moberly on the other; we may adopt the more moderate conclusions of Lightfoot or Hort. But whatever line we take, we shall

feel no doubt that in our own country the
Ministry of the Church of England answers
more nearly than any other to the Ministry
in the New Testament. The Church of
England is historically the successor of the
earliest Churches in this land, and as regards
authoritative ministry, whatever be the case
with other bodies, her position is unassailable.
Your minds are probably at rest on that point.
You feel perhaps more certain in what Church
you will exercise your ministry than whether
you shall exercise a ministry at all. If called
at all, you are called to the ministry of the
Church of England. But it may be more
difficult to decide whether you are called at
all. And if you have no vocation to the
ministry, you cannot expect a sense of mission
in your work as a minister.

The Church of England requires you to be
clear on both these points. She charges her
Bishops to ask the candidates for Ordination
these questions :

" Do you trust that you are inwardly moved
by the Holy Ghost to take upon you this Office
and Ministration, to serve God for the promoting
of His glory, and the edifying of His people ? "

" Do you think that you are truly called,
according to the Will of our Lord Jesus

Christ, and the due order of this Realm, to the Ministry of the Church?"

As to what constitutes vocation it is difficult to say exactly. Doubtless it is largely of a subjective nature. It is to some the call of a voice which seems to speak within, which they believe to be that of the Holy Spirit. Some of the ancient prophets were called in this way. Amos was a herdman and gatherer of sycamore fruit (Amos vii. 14). He was engaged in his usual avocations when God called him, "Go, prophesy unto My people Israel" (vii. 15). Where this assurance is absent, it must be difficult to decide whether one has a vocation, but its absence does not determine the question. And the Church does not require absolute certainty on either point from the candidates for the Ministry. "I trust so," "I think so," are the replies to the two questions. There may be the honest conviction that one is so led or moved, without the apparent speaking of a voice. But where this conviction is wanting, a sense of the needs of the world and a fancied taste for the work are scarcely sufficient to constitute vocation, especially if one be settled in another calling. Yet the coincidence of these with other factors may go far to settle the matter. Early aversion to the work of the Ministry may give place to interest; interest may grow to love; and love may evoke a desire for a call. This desire—if one's motives be sincere—may be the prompting of the Holy Ghost. There may also come in due succession the removal of difficulties; consent of parents or responsible persons; provision of means for preparation; acceptance by a College as a member, or by a Bishop as a candidate.

At the same time some who are so far on towards admission to Holy Orders as membership of the Theological Faculty of this College implies, may still feel or may begin to feel some doubts as to vocation. Do not be alarmed at this. It is better to feel diffidence than to shew presumption. And such hesitation may be a sign of true vocation after all. It may come from that sense of unworthiness which has always marked the best of God's servants, even Moses and Isaiah, St. Peter and St. Paul. But if increased light and accurate self-examination make one certain of the want of vocation, it is better to draw back even at the twelfth hour than to put one's hand mistakenly to the plough. Even then the step of withdrawal should not be taken without seeking the guidance of God

and the counsel of those of His servants who
are most competent to judge and to advise.

Most of "you have well weighed and
pondered these things with yourselves long
before this time." You have passed beyond
the stages of uncertainty or preliminary inquiry.
These questions have been settled ere you
came here, and settled more definitely than
is the case with many theological students
and candidates for Holy Orders at our older
universities. And though it may do you no
harm to review your position and your experience, yet most of you will feel little unsettlement in so doing. For the call has come
to not a few of you, as it came to St. Matthew,
to forsake business life and to give up your
whole time to the Ministry of the Gospel.
You have obeyed the call—in some cases
after years of thought, prayer and inquiry.
For a time perhaps ways and means were
not available. But even this difficulty was
providential. For it tested your determina-
tion, it proved your vocation ; and its removal
enabled you to answer the question and to
obey the call to become Fishers of Men and
Shepherds of Souls. "You have clearly deter-
mined, by God's grace, to give yourselves
wholly to this Office, whereunto it hath pleased

God to call you." Though not in other
respects quite ready to enter the work of the
Ministry, you can already answer in anticipa-
tion the two questions of the Bishop to whom
you will present yourselves for ordination.

At present nearly all of you are still laymen. Thank God for this. It is, of course,
quite right that you should be longing for
the day of ordination to arrive, and for the
years of ministry to begin, but you have
still the opportunity of rightly using the office
of a layman. Do not undervalue the importance of the ministry of the laity. The office
of the clergy—St. Paul tells us—is to set
the limbs of the Body of Christ to fulfil their
proper functions—" for the perfecting of the
Saints, unto the work of ministering, unto the
building up of the Body of Christ " (Ephesians
iv. 12, R.V.). Excellent and useful Christian
work is open to and is being done by laymen.

Often so soon as a man engaged in some
profession is converted to God, his thoughts
turn towards the Ministry. If led in that
direction his experience of life as a layman
will be of great use. The late Bishop Selwyn
—as Canon Wilson says happily in one of
his sermons—" was everything in his Southern
diocese, admiral, cook, diver, groom, as well

as scholar and pastor of souls, and was the
better bishop because he was so much else"
(*Cambridge Review*, October 23rd, 1890).

It would not, however, be well for all laymen whose spiritual consciousness is awakened
by the Holy Spirit to aspire to Holy Orders.
The desire of many for ordination may proceed
from true love of work for souls.   In some
few cases it may be prompted by the fond
fancy that the clerical life is one of less temptation and of less difficulty than the lay.   Even
where this notion is cherished, the motive may
be quite pure.   But God wants many men to
remain where they are after their conversion.
Rudyard Kipling's cattle-drover might have
aspired to the ministry, if he had been of
higher social position.   As it was he naturally
shrank from going back to serve Christ among
the rough and ungodly men employed in the
cattle-boats.   But his conversion was sincere,
and when God's will for him was made plain,
Mulholland proved true to his Contract :

" An' I spoke to God of our Contract, an' He says to
        my prayer :
' I never puts on My ministers no more than they can
        bear.
    So back you go to the cattle-boats an' preach My
        Gospel there.'

I didn't want to do it, for I knew what I should get,
An' I wanted to preach Religion, handsome an' out of
   the wet,
But the Word of the Lord were lain on me, an' I
   done what I was set."

           (*Seven Seas*—" Mulholland's Contract.")

A layman may be occupying a position which involves grave difficulties to a consistently Christian man ; it may be his duty, as it was Mulholland's, to remain there. And it cannot be doubted that avenues of usefulness are open to the layman which the clergyman cannot enter. A layman of faithful life and of straightforward character may be of the utmost blessing in his own calling. His spare time he may largely devote to what we technically call Christian work—perhaps more popularly Church work. Large fields of service amongst men, lads and boys he will find open. He may espouse the cause of Foreign Missions. He may throw himself into the current of Church life. He may take his share in the counsels of the Church ; first in inferior and later in more prominent branches of her Councils. And I have not mentioned the cause of social reform, or the work of local or national administration in which he may prove of great service. He may, moreover, exercise a general Christian influence. In these days the mere knowledge that a man of probity is on the side of Christ counts for something in his office or in local circles of society. His attitude will cause men of serious inclination to think. Further, he will be able to bear specific testimony to Christ. Times will occur when he can quietly warn some brother who is fast going down hill, or draw some one who seems in need of help closer to his Master.

Learn then to set the highest value on the life and influence of laymen. You may thereby be able to cheer some of your own friends who crave but lack the special opportunity which God has placed within your reach.

Your appreciation of the office of a layman will help you to rightly regard the Churchmen of the parish where you will soon be called to minister. It will also lead you to fulfil the important ministry of the laity until you yourselves are admitted to the Diaconate.

The notion that a layman can do more good than a clergyman obtains in some quarters even of Christian belief and life. It may be fostered by the faults and peculiarities of some clergymen. But it stands to reason

c

that the duties of most laymen require them to devote most of their time and the best of their energies to their daily business. A clergyman, if faithful to the Pastoral idea, spends his whole time in promoting the Kingdom of God. His freshest powers, his best thought, his keenest faculties are devoted to that object. And he can help and direct those very laymen whose desire is to spend and be spent in the service of God. The consecration of a man's whole time and strength to the work of the ministry is a corrective to the spirit of the age, which assumes that the main purpose of life is to make money and to enjoy the world, to get on and to get honour. The highest privilege is surely to serve and to bless. The Divine view still remains, and to those who accept the New Testament the Christian Ministry must be the highest calling open to man, to be prized above all others by those who are privileged to enter it, to be esteemed very highly for its work's sake by those to whom its ministrations extend.

How will you spend the few months of service which are still left to you as laymen? "Set in order the things that are wanting, strengthen the things which remain." Aim at being found faithful.   Do not take a share in Church work with the mere wish to become expert in 'the things appertaining to the Ecclesiastical Administration,' or versed in details of ritual. While you are a layman, be a layman. A clerical layman does not command much influence. Do not take up Church work because you are hoping to be a clergyman, but make yourself useful to men for the sake of and as a servant of Christ.

Remember that if a man is of little use as a layman he will be of still less as a clergyman. " He that is faithful in that which is least, is faithful also in much : and he that is unjust in the least, is unjust also in much " (St. Luke xvi. 10).

Spontaneous Christian service as a layman will help you to avoid pedantry and professionalism as a clergyman.   Perhaps those are most happily situated whose energies are thrown into Christ's service before the thought of seeking Holy Orders comes into the mind.

To the need of a sincere share in Church work may I add that of helping men in your own station of life ? Mission to a humbler class is easier than mission to one's own rank. And the stamp of man who is scarcely known in religious connection to men of his own

acquaintance as more than a Christian man
or a potential clergyman is not to be commended. A word must be given for the Lord,
when opportunity offers, to relations, friends
or acquaintances, who profess indifference to
the claims of Christ. We must not speak
as if spiritually or morally superior to them.
There may be more desire for grace in their
hearts than they allow to appear on the
surface. But while an unreal word to them
would savour of cant, and a word of lofty
superiority would mark one as a prig, a word
spoken in love will not often be resented. Not
to speak at all may be selfish or cowardly.

Do not forget the importance of spiritual
intercourse with your friends who are like-
minded, whether engaged in lay callings, or
preparing to enter the ministry. You will
readily understand that this does not mean
talking clerical 'shop' or ecclesiastical gossip.
That may become positively pernicious. Very
different is conversation on the work of God,
on your own difficulties and perplexities; on
the means of overcoming temptations; on the
help received from the Lord through means of
grace; on the progress of the Kingdom of
God; on the victory of the love of Christ over
a single soul; on experience of God's dealings

with the soul—to use an old-fashioned but suggestive phrase ; on the absence or presence of devotion to the Redeemer.

It is well if such words will come, and if they come from hearts which burn.   But if the heart does not burn, when the words are spoken, the Saviour will hearken and hear, He will draw near, He will teach and inspire, He will reveal Himself.   And then we shall know that it was good to be there, and that our hearts did burn within us, while Jesus Himself drew near and went with us.   Now is the time when, if ever, such words are to come.   Well does the author of *Pastor Pastorum* describe the early inter-course of the five Apostles whose call is recorded in the first chapter of St. John's gospel—" baring their hearts each to the other in the confidence of youth" (p. 156).   Such occasions are sacred, and they are not always at our command.   For such words must be natural and spontaneous.   An old Harrow master used to say to his boys : " Be natural in spiritual things, and you will then be spiritual in natural things."

The speaking of what Archbishop Alexander in a beautiful passage (*Primary Convictions*, Discussion iv. p. 111) calls a 'religious word' will not only help you at the time, it will have another outcome. It will soon be your duty to speak to others, both religious and non-religious, of the things of God. You will wish to be instant in season and out of season. What impression will your words make, if they be spoken in a forced and artificial manner, merely as a matter of duty? They will not carry conviction to the hearer's heart. Their unreality may deflect the hearer's thoughts from himself to yourself. If, however, you breathe the atmosphere of heaven, and are not strangers to its language and conversation at other times, your words will be spoken fitly and will be felt to come from the heart. Even if your testimony be rejected, hearers will recognize that God is in you of a truth and will take knowledge of you that you have been with Jesus. Dwell with the King for His work, and He will dwell with you in yours. And as at the Incarnation God the Son stooped to earthly surroundings of the humblest type, so He will stoop to enter your heart as you seek to fulfil in your life the purpose of the Incarnation, and He will manifest Himself to you and through you to others.

The period through which you are now passing is of great importance to yourselves. Regard it not merely as a time to be got

through before you can take up definite work,
or even as a time for acquiring sufficient information to pass the required examinations, but
far more as a time of intercourse with God in
preparation for the solemn work which He is
calling upon you to undertake.   Let this be
your Arabia where, like St. Paul, you retire to
learn more of the counsel of God for yourself,
for the church and for the world ; and where
after communion with the Good Shepherd you
will understand more clearly the idea of the
Pastorate and will be more ready to receive
His commission to feed and to tend His flock.

II.

THE PASTOR'S INNER LIFE.

In my first Lecture I spoke of the almost impatience which one is tempted to feel at the time of waiting for the work of the Ministry to begin. One longs to plunge into the midst of life's work, but one has to wait a while. You may, perhaps, entertain similar feelings with regard to the subjects of these lectures. You would prefer to enter at once into the details of practical work rather than to spend further time over what may appear to be but preliminaries to the actual subject. But in devoting two lectures out of ten to the vocation and inner life of the Pastor, I am following distinguished lead. Canon Liddon opens his book on *Clerical Life and Work* with the following remarks: "It is a matter for just complaint with candidates for holy orders, that many books which profess to treat of pastoral work address themselves almost exclusively to the external duties of the Christian Priest. They enter at length upon a consideration of such points as the composition of sermons, visiting the sick, schools, ritual; and they continually insist upon the necessity of bringing the inward life to bear upon the discharge of such outward and visible ministries. The existence of an inward life is indeed assumed, but no attempt is made to determine its specific character, or the laws of its formation." If Canon Liddon's criticism be correct, these manuals begin with a series of presuppositions, which they somewhat too readily take for granted. With some of these I propose to deal in this Lecture.

When we read the history of the early Church, we are impressed by the demeanour of the Christians in times of severe persecution. They possessed few of our advantages. They lacked many confirmations of the faith which are well known to us. They had to endure excruciating tortures and cruel forms of death. Yet they faced their trials without flinching. Many longed for the martyr's crown. And in the midst of suffering their souls were filled with joy.

The same note of triumph marked the exodus from bondage of many brave men, women, and children in the Marian persecutions. If the spirits of some failed, other sufferers would cheer them. " Be of good comfort, Master Ridley, and play the man. We shall this day light such a candle, by God's grace, in England, as I trust shall never be put out."

This note of joy is not so characteristic of the present age. But to what can we ascribe its absence? Perhaps we rejoice less because we suffer less. Dr. Jowett in his sermon on Bunyan and Spinoza remarks: "There is more toleration, more knowledge than formerly; but is there the same heroism, the same self-sacrifice, the same intensity, the same elevation of character, the same aspiration after an ideal life, the same death to the world, the same continued struggle for the good of man? People ask, who would be a martyr nowadays? and the sting of the jest lies in the truth of it" (*Sermons Biographical and Miscellaneous*, p. 46).

We are frequently told that the present age witnesses the decay of conviction. Our candid friend—the *Hibbert Journal*, our avowed enemies, and even our avowed friends amongst the press, tell us this. If this be true we can explain the decay of joy. It has been said that conviction built Cathedrals; it was certainly conviction which gave martyrs and confessors their spiritual power and joy.

The decay of conviction may be due to the shaking of the foundations of the faith, to the questioning of every settled belief, to the regarding of nothing as certain. General unsettlement does prevail. " Men's hearts failing them for fear, and for looking after those things which are coming on the earth " (St. Luke xxi. 26).

Some share must be ascribed to the spirit of the world, which is ever ready to invade the Church. And certainly there is not the same separation from the world on the part of earnest folk as once there was. Doubtless the definition of the world and of worldliness was somewhat too artificial a generation or two back, but there was something to be said for the policy, if not for the logic of our grand-parents. We, however, are too ready to enjoy the pleasures of the world, to be on good terms with the world, even to love the world—and by the world I mean that section of society which leaves God out of account. And we are too apt to forget that the same world which crucified our Lord once would crucify Him again.

This decay of conviction may co-exist with great activity on the part of the Church. The machinery of ecclesiastical organization may be working on all sides. The stones of new churches may be continually rising. The bells of existing churches may be continuously ringing. Yet there may be absence of true spiritual life, power and joy.

What marks the Church may mark the individual pastor. He may be exact and accurate, smart and up-to-date, capable and business-like, true and just, courteous and considerate, energetic, hard-working, pains-taking and self-denying. Yet he may lack spiritual life and power. His training may be excellent, his scholarship may be quite good, his credentials may be unimpeachable, his orders may be unquestioned, yet he may not be capable of winning men to God, he may not even have the joy of the Lord as his own strength.

In this connection Archbishop Benson contrasts δύναμις with ἐξουσία. In his charge entitled *Fishers of Men*, he says: "Our Lord taught and worked with 'authority' as well as with 'power,' and the Apostles received

' power' as well as authority, and the Christian clerus ought to have both." After stating how "in sinful times 'power' has departed from 'authority' and has reappeared" elsewhere, he proceeds, "what so hollow as for authority to have to vindicate itself conscious of departed power? But alas! the man feels it must be done, and so does an institution. . . . Gradually the service of religion is mechanised, and even then it is so soothing and so fair, as it gently becomes more material and sensuous, that it is delighted in. It is even a kind of conscientiousness which searches for working substitutes when the acquisition and exercise of that real spiritual power which lies in the awful contact with Christ's holiness and judgment is too painful and constant." [1]

This power is the gift of the Holy Spirit alone, but it is largely connected with conviction. Now the word 'conviction' suggests by derivation 'conquest,' and its primary meaning is concerned—as Murray says—with "The proving or finding a person guilty of an offence with which he is charged before a legal tribunal; legal proof or declaration

[1] Quoted by Dr. A. W. Robinson in his *Personal Life of the Clergy*, appendix. (Longmans, 1904.)

of guilt." May we not combine these ideas
and say that conviction has specially to
do with man's shortcomings? He realizes
what sin is in itself, that is, as God sees it.
God's law comes home to him, conquers, over-
comes, convicts him. Then he sees how the
Lamb of God has taken away the sin of the
world. His own conscience is satisfied by
the Cross. And Christ now appeals to him
with irresistible power, and conquers him
completely; He carries away his whole
being. The conquest of love becomes conviction in the general sense. Nothing can
shake it.

It must not be supposed that the conviction
of sin leading up to strong conviction in
general depends on the degree to which one
has sinned. A man who in the eyes of the
world had not sinned at all might be most
deeply convinced of sin. While another who
had drunk deeply of the poisoned cup might
say with little more than dread of possible
consequences, "I have sinned." In many
cases it must be said, as was said of Werner
by Carlyle, "His belief is likely to have been
persuasion rather than conviction." We long
for this powerful conviction. We cannot be
faithful in ministry without it.

Mr. Dimock in some recent comments on Isaiah vi. 5 well sums up our present position : "What a word of caution for any one who may be tempted to say 'Here I am' before humbly submitting to receive the conviction of sin, . . . before hearing by faith the word, 'Lo, thine iniquity is taken away, and thy sin purged!' Should not the conscience first be touched by a live coal from the true altar of redeeming love, and then be ready to say, 'Send me'?" (*The Record*, October 28th, 1904, p. 1105).

For the deepening of conviction we need to ask God to shew us more clearly what He is. The more lofty our view of His holiness, the deeper will be our conviction of sin. The meaning of the Cross will become clearer. We shall know that in virtue of our Saviour's Passion and Death our sins are forgiven, and that it is with a Risen and Ascended Christ—that is, a Living Christ—that we have to do. We shall expect and receive from Him grace to conquer sin day by day.

The Apostles were men who had companied with our Blessed Lord and were witnesses of His Resurrection. And if you aspire to be successors of the Apostles in any sense, you must be able to speak from personal experience of your knowledge of Christ and of what He has done and is doing for your soul. Your Churchmanship may be good, your knowledge of theology fair, but at the root of everything—if you are to do the least good as a clergyman—must lie the personal experience of deliverance by the Living Christ from the guilt and power of sin. This must mean severance from sin in your own heart. If a candidate for Holy Orders is the victim of secret temptation, if sin in any form has the dominion over him, he is belying the power of the Gospel, and condemning his ministry to hopeless failure.

The man who knows what Christ has done and is doing for him, and who in His strength has broken with wilful and conscious sin, can look with clear conscience into the face of God in Christ. And he who can look into the face of Christ can look into the face of man. And when you can look man in the face without flinching, you will have power with men and will prevail. You will have a single eye, a single heart, and a single aim. Men will see that you have a strength of which they know not, a strength which comes by faith in Jesus Christ. "This is the victory

that overcometh the world, even our faith"
(1 St. John v. 4).

This will lift our belief up from the sphere
of opinion to that of conviction. People come
asking, What am I to believe? as if ready
to accept anything which may be put before
them and thinking that the holding of certain
opinions carries with it salvation. And with
the confusion of belief with opinion comes the
notion on the part of others that they may pick
and choose what to believe—the root idea of
heresy—and that degenerates into the idea that
it does not matter what one believes. But
belief is much more than opinion. It is something which affects one's whole conduct, and
to which the inner consciousness responds.

Do not be afraid of the charge that your
religion is too subjective. Personal religion
is not a mere matter of emotion, or of feeling; yet one great testimony to the truth of
Christianity is the response which its doctrines
evoke from the individual soul. Taken as a
theory merely and tested at every point of
experience and in many thousands of cases,
the Gospel does not break down.

You will not, however, allow your spiritual
life to be one-sided. The objective side of
religion will be kept in view as well as the

D

subjective. The two sides are complementary.
They may be summed up in the phrases—
'the Faith' and 'faith.' The Church has
been tempted to lay stress now on one, now
on the other. The right course is to keep
both in their proper places. The historic and
the common faith once delivered to the saints
must be contended for. But in virtue of it
the individual man must exercise personal
faith in Christ. Some years ago one of our
diocesan bishops wrote to me: "I used to
think that faith was preached too exclusively,
and now I think we are ignoring it a great
deal in the pulpit. Is pendulum the only
motion the world knows?"

Surely the Church of England occupies a
strong position here. She holds *the* faith as
firmly as Rome could claim to do, and at the
same time insists on the necessity of personal
faith, not ascribing to the Sacraments or other
means of grace the automatic results which
on Rome's theory seem to follow. On the
other hand she insists on *faith* as keenly
as any Nonconformist, who—in the Bishop's
words—may have preached faith too exclusively, but she does not confound faith with
assurance, nor does she treat the articles of the
faith as open to question. Here in the Church

of England is common ground, on which the reunion of the Churches at any rate of western Christendom—if ever it is to take place—may become an accomplished fact.

Like Church, like Churchman—we may again observe. What is true of the corporate body, should be true of the individual member. The faith must be held fast, regarded as an objective whole ; not wrapped in a napkin, but tested, tried and lived by every day of one's life.

I do not dwell at greater length on the importance of holding fast to the elements of the faith, not because the subject is of second importance, but because I have in view the inner life of the Christian Minister. It is possible to be thoroughly orthodox, to accord to the faith full intellectual assent, and yet to be little affected in heart or life by the details of the faith. And I doubt whether the position which the Church accords to faith in the sense of personal trust in God is sufficiently appreciated by Churchmen at large. Faith is associated with the Sacraments in the Liturgy, the Catechism and the Articles. Faith comes in with every experience of religious life. Conversion, regeneration, renewal, vocation, self-surrender and mission have much to do with faith. But we shall avoid the mistake of supposing that faith is a purely subjective quality, the amount of which we possess largely affects our spiritual welfare. Our faith may be as small as a grain of mustard seed, yet it can remove mountains if placed in the right Person—our Blessed Lord Himself. Faith will enable a man to go further than accept the Incarnation, the Cross, the Resurrection as facts; faith will connect these truths with himself. Faith will enable a man to say, 'The Lord Jesus is our Saviour'; it will enable him to go further, 'The Lord Jesus is *my* Saviour.' It is strange that some earnest souls seem unable to come so far. The Lord is their own Saviour, and they are trusting in Him alone, yet they hesitate to say so much. This does not mean loss of salvation or loss of privilege. But it does mean loss of power and of effectiveness as a Christian force in the world. Certainty here helps one to speak with confidence and to reach individual souls.

We may again turn Carlyle to account, "At all times a man who would do faithfully must believe firmly."

Do not shrink from this as pointing to an unduly individualist religion. We do not forget that ours is the Catholic religion. But here again the balance of truth must be held. As with the objective and the subjective, with the Faith and faith, so with the collective or Catholic and the individual. Both must be kept in view. Our religion—and specially the religion of the clergyman—must be individualist. The clergyman must himself be personally right with God, and must know that he is right. And he must seek souls individually; they cannot be won to God in the mass. Our Lord himself while ministering to the multitudes at large, bestowed great care on individual souls, and attached them one by one to His cause. You will not then depreciate the individualist side of religion, however zealous you may be in the cause of catholicity. True catholicity does not exclude individualism. I once heard a clergyman read a paper on the 'Catholicity of the Order for Morning Prayer.' He urged that there was no place in the office for the *expression* of individual worship. He managed to explain away the person and the number used in the recitation of the Apostles' Creed. But he quite forgot that the Te Deum—after calling on the universe and the Church to praise God, and ascribing worship to each Person of the Trinity, concludes with the

personal needs of the individual worshipper :
"O Lord, in Thee have I trusted ; let me
never be confounded." We do not quarrel
over the plea for the Catholicity of the Daily
Office, but we object to a one-sided and
exclusive view of the matter. We can afford
to lose sight of neither the corporate nor the
individual aspect in our worship and our
work. Rightly divide the word of truth, and
hold the balance between the various elements
which compose it.

We must remember also the place of *hope*
in the life of the individual soul. We are
undertaking difficult work, if we realize that
our duty is to bring men to God, and to raise
the whole tone of our parishes. Anyone can
pay visits, read services, conduct marriages and
burials, preach sermons and answer letters—
after a fashion. But it is not everyone who
can in the discharge of these duties lift men
up to God. Spiritual life does not come
naturally, and even where men are influenced,
persecution, the cares of this world, or the
deceitfulness of riches operate powerfully to
check the growth of the seed sown. When men
and women settle down in life, their characters
soon get fixed, and it seems almost impossible
to change them. Those who are without God

are described as 'without hope in the world';
despair takes hold of them; they think that
it is of no good to attempt to be different and
they have no desire to try. Yet we are sent
to bring new life to our parishes, perhaps to
foster what does not exist. A clergyman in
South London once complained to Bishop
Thorold that he could do so little in his parish
because he found so little spiritual interest
there. "But I thought you were sent there
to create it," was the Bishop's ready reply.
Here is our difficulty. How are we to meet
it? I have already spoken of the need of faith;
we must have faith that God is able and
willing to use us to meet the difficulty. But
we must also have hope. What do we mean
by hope? and what is its scope?

In the New Testament the word 'hope'
seems to be used in three connections. There
is (1) *the* hope, the definite, the particular hope
which the Christian possesses—"Christ in you,
the hope of glory" (Colossians i. 27). This
hope relates mainly to the world to come.
We must possess this hope, and know it.
(2) The hope of heaven should lead to a
hoping for heaven. Here—as I hinted in my
opening lecture [1]—the present generation of

[1] See page 15.

Christians is defective. We are not heavenly-minded enough. We are too content with the world as it is. We know that when the time comes, we shall have a right to enter heaven. But we do not look forward to that entrance as we should do. It would not be natural for us to wish to leave the world one day before our work is done. We are sent into the world to do a certain work, and God means us to desire to accomplish it. But if we were worn out with labours for the Master, if we endured severe persecution for His sake, we should probably anticipate the realization of *the* hope more than we do. We ought not to be un-natural, still less unreal, in the hopes which we cherish or express. But at any rate the hope of heaven ought to make us ready to leave the world at any time. And even if we do not hope for the time to come soon for us to arrive in heaven, we ought to hope that the time will come soon for our Lord to arrive on earth.

(3) The possession of *the* hope and the look-ing forward to its realization should lead to a Divine hopefulness on the part of the messenger of Christ. He comes with good news, with a message of hope, and he approaches his people with hopeful heart, hopeful manner and hopeful tone. A dejected

spirit and a doleful voice will never win any man, and even when dealing with the most hardened or the most sinful we must remember that there is hope for their souls. Though some day it may be too late to mend, it is not too late to-day. This hopefulness is not a cheery optimism which some men of the world may possess as a matter of temperament. It will not be enough for us to bid men to cheer up and to make the best of things, unless we can tell them something more. My predecessor in my present post adopted as his parish motto for the year 1900 the marginal reading of two verses in the Revised Version—" Brighten up." But there was something about his very manner which shewed men the best way to brighten up. And when a few months later he was killed by a fall from his bicycle in Scotland, the recollection of what he had known and taught helped the people to live up to the motto he had given them. The hope which we wish to see spring up in men's hearts is an eternal hope, based on certainty—the dwelling of Christ in the individual soul.

Yet again there is a requisite without which no man can do the work of the ministry—*love*. It was love which brought our Lord into the world. It was His love which drew us first to

Him. The conviction of sin shewed us our need. We saw in Christ the Saviour whom we needed. Our love, however cold and faint, responded to His love. Now He sends us forth as His Ministers to tell of His love. The first requisite in our approach to the Lord may be faith. "Without faith it is impossible to please Him : for he that cometh to God must believe that He is, and that He is a rewarder of them that diligently seek Him" (Hebrews xi. 6). St. Paul places faith first in the three graces of faith, hope and love, but he says that the greatest of these is love. And the power of love is a grander mark of the minister of Christ than the love of power. Of a well-known clergyman it was said by a friend : "The source and centre of his power was the great love that filled his heart." The greatest factor in the world's redemption is love. God is love, and it was only in keeping with His character that He should so love the world as to send His only-begotten Son into the world to redeem mankind. The love of God in Christ is not realized by thousands of men and women even in a Christian country, but many are awakened to know what the love of Christ is to the world in general, and to themselves in particular. This is often preceded by a sense of sin, and it is not to be wondered at that an age in which the sense of sin is strangely deficient—as so observant a thinker as Mr. Gladstone stated— should witness a decline in devotion to our Lord. " To whom little is forgiven, the same loveth little " (St. Luke vii. 47). One remedy for this will be to preach the Law, but in this lecture we are chiefly concerned with our own spiritual life, so let us be careful to preach the Law to ourselves, that our consciences may be quickened, and our hearts may know what the love of Christ is to us. " We love Him, because He first loved us " (1 St. John iv. 19).

We can trace the working of these laws in the spiritual experience of many of God's people in former generations. The religious revival of the eighteenth century was marked by a personal devotion to our Lord which gave rise to every kind of good work, to willing endurance of obloquy and persecution, of suffering and affliction. It has been so since, and it will be the case again. We may take for granted that deeper views of our own sinfulness will lead to increased devotion to Christ. And for the heart to be full of love for Christ cannot fail to have a stimulating effect on our ministrations and to increase in us that enthusiasm without which—Bishop Westcott says—youth will lead to maturity without faith, and to old age without hope (*Incarnation and Common Life*). But we must not rest satisfied with mere emotion however sincere and however comforting. The response of our love to the constraining love of Christ will be shewn in hatred for what opposed Him and love for what He taught and for those whom He loved. Therefore devotion to our Lord cannot exist side by side with the toleration of any sin. If our consciences allow us to continue in any one sin while professing allegiance to Christ, we may conclude that our appreciation of the Saviour is more a desire to escape the consequences of sin in virtue of His Cross, than a true and genuine love for Him. There must also be with love for our Lord love for what He loves. That Christians have not always shewn such love is attested by the long delay in carrying out His last command to the Church—to preach the Gospel to every creature. It is recognized also in the prayer of our Church that we may love that which the Lord commands as well as obtain that which He promises.

With true love for Christ will also come deep love for souls. It is hard to define what love for souls is. That love causes the shepherd to take endless trouble in his search for one lost sheep.   It is the very essence of the pastoral gift.   Love for our Lord on the one hand, and on the other love for the souls for whom He died connect us with God and man, and give us greater power to bring men to God.   This love gives a man that sympathy which draws out the affections of others, and helps many a cripple over the stiles on life's pathway.   But my present concern is with our own inner spiritual life, so I leave this branch of the subject.   We can examine ourselves as to whether we possess this true love for our Lord, as evidenced by its fruits.   We ought not merely to take up those things which are near our Lord's heart, because it is right to do so. We ought to wish to do so.   Foreign missions, for instance, ought to be of absorbing interest to us, not because of any romance in such missions, nor because of their record of wonderful work or heroic self-sacrifice, nor because of the interesting character of *some* modern missionary magazines, but because our Lord is waiting for the gospel to be proclaimed to all nations, and because He died for the millions of heathen who have not yet heard His Name.   If our hearts are not yet completely won by the love of Christ, we shall find here a cause of spiritual inefficiency when we enter upon parochial work. The constraining motive will be absent, and our ministry will be sadly impaired. But one thing may be wanting without which all else is of little avail. "Though I bestow all my goods to feed the poor, and though I give my body to be burned, and have not charity, it profiteth me nothing" (1 Corinthians xiii. 3). These words of St. Paul have their application to-day, when there is unending work in our large parishes. Even in spite of our boasted Church life, it may be questioned whether the Christ life in the Church is what it has been in days gone by.

The acknowledgment of this defect is not a reason for looking back from the plough to which you have put your hand. It is a reason for deep searching of heart and for earnest prayer. Of course, from one point of view the Holy Spirit alone can revive our souls and quicken in our hearts the flame of sacred love. But from another point of view the remedy lies largely in your own hands. "Keep yourselves in the love of God" (St. Jude 21). St. Jude speaks very solemnly of the addiction of some professing Christians—and Christian teachers too —to sensual sin. But our duty is plain—to keep ourselves unspotted from the world,

and to build up ourselves on our most holy
faith, praying in the Holy Ghost. Daily
attention to the walk with God, daily study
of the Word of God, daily confession and
prayer to God have much to do with keeping
ourselves in His love. Allow time for that
love ever to penetrate your soul afresh. Its
stores are like those of the grace of God—
ever fresh and new. If we speak from personal
experience in these matters, we shall have a
message and we shall not lack hearers. In
the earliest days men who had companied
with the Lord Jesus and were witnesses of
His Resurrection were chosen to fill vacancies
in the list of the Apostles. In these days
though we have not seen with our eyes the
Lord Jesus after the flesh, our experience and
our knowledge are no less real.

The man who has reached this stage may
without fear profess himself converted. Do
not be afraid of the word conversion. Though
much has been read into the word which does
not rightly pertain to it, the word represents
a spiritual reality. It has been confused with
regeneration. The two are really quite distinct. Conversion has been erected into so
fixed a type of spiritual emotion, that its
accidents have come to be mistaken for

conversion itself. And a mistake has been made in describing conversion as if it were the working of some influence which is brought to bear on the soul from without. But the word suffers from the disability attaching to the use of a technical term in religious phraseology. So long as a word in current use is employed to denote some religious experience or doctrine, the popular meaning of the word will help to correct any deviation from its proper meaning in religious language. But let a word stand by itself, so to speak, in such language, and it may slip from one meaning to another—in fact may acquire almost any meaning in course of time. The word 'conversion' having thus acquired a meaning of its own, the Revisers of the English Bible have perhaps done well to eliminate almost altogether the word from the Revised Version of the New Testament, and to give the simpler word 'turn' in its place. A survey of the passages in the New Testament, where the Greek equivalents of the word 'conversion' or 'converted' occur, shews that in each case the Greek verb occurs in the active voice. We thus learn that the word 'convert' simply means to turn to God, and the word 'conversion' the act of turning to God. For instance, in the well-known quotation from Isaiah (vi. 9) the Revised Version in St. Matthew xiii. 15 reads :

> "Lest haply they should perceive with their eyes,
> And hear with their ears,
> And understand with their heart,
> And should turn again,
> And I should heal them."

St. Peter preaching at Jerusalem said, "Repent ye therefore and turn again, that your sins may be blotted out" (Acts iii. 19, R.V.). Such are a few from many instances of the use of the word for that initial turning to God which we call conversion. But inasmuch as turning to God may take place many times in a man's life, though a man who has once turned to the Lord ought never to turn away from Him, the same word is used of St. Peter's recovery after his denial. In St. Luke xxii. 32, R.V., we read, "But I made supplication for thee, that thy faith fail not : and do thou, when once thou has turned again, stablish thy brethren." In one instance the word is used of the turning of another to God, and there the word 'convert' is retained ;—"He which converteth a sinner from the error of his way shall save a soul from death, and shall hide a multitude of

E

sins" (St. James v. 20, R.V.). In all these
cases the word is used in the sense which it
bears in common life—"Turn again, Whittington, Lord Mayor of London." The same
word is used in the account of the raising
of Dorcas by St. Peter: "Peter put them
all forth, and kneeled down, and prayed; and
turning to the body, he said, Tabitha, arise"
(Acts ix. 40, R.V.).

The New Testament removes the ground
from many wrong notions concerning conversion, but this fact must not tempt us to
forget to emphasize the necessity of conversion
itself. There must be a definite turning to
God on our own part, and we must look for
such turning to God on the part of those to
whom we minister. The step may be gradual,
or it may be the act of a moment. And the
test of our having taken it is the direction in
which we face at the present time. We are
told that the Samaritans in a certain village
would not receive our Lord, "because His
face was as though He were going to Jerusalem" (St. Luke ix. 53, R.V.). Is it as
clear to the men of the world to-day that our
faces are set in the direction of the Heavenly
Jerusalem, the City of the Great King? Do
not rely on your Baptism merely, or your

Baptismal privileges. The Bishop of Birmingham in a sermon at Westminster Abbey (March 25th, 1895), thus expressed this truth. " Baptism will not make you good ; not all the sacraments will make you good. . . . But except ye be converted, except ye turn and become as little children, except with that deliberate turning you welcome and accept the grace which He puts at your disposal, never shall you know what is the meaning of that regenerate life, and what is conversion. In some cases it is sudden. . . . But in the majority of cases the process is a gradual one. But, be it sudden or be it gradual, it is not the less necessary."

Bishop Gore reminds us of the distinction between conversion and regeneration. The exact definition of regeneration is a question which admits of considerable discussion, but speaking broadly we may say that conversion is the act of the man himself, and regeneration the act of the Holy Ghost. But whatever view we take of the scope of the word regeneration, we shall not be tempted to give it too wide a range. Regeneration does not produce a mature Christian. The result of the new birth is in any given case a babe in Christ. And growth and progress are to continue until the babe becomes τέλειος. This progress of the soul is described by the term 'renewal,' which implies not only a growth or development of powers implanted by the Holy Spirit, but also a replenishment of spiritual vigour impaired by the wear and tear of life; and a gradual replacement of phases of our sinful nature with the result that instead of being carnal we become spiritual. The Collect for Christmas day sums up what should be our experience : " Grant that we being regenerate, and made Thy children by adoption and grace, may daily be renewed by Thy Holy Spirit."

The mere possession of these blessings is a priceless boon, but they mean more to a man now if he *knows* that he has them. What power and progress would mark our spiritual life if we could only take the bold step of recognizing what we have in Christ, and of daring to say so. Amongst the laity much ground is lost by shortcoming here. But when clergymen cannot state plainly what the Lord has done and is doing for their souls, can they expect to see definite spiritual progress in the life of those whom they teach? But I do not wish to take the utilitarian stand-point. By all means have an eye to everything which will increase your usefulness as ministers of Christ; but think also of the best gifts, which all laymen ought to covet, and of that standard which God asks and can enable all Christians to reach. If you are not in spiritual experience all that laymen ought to be, are you fit to be entrusted with the office of a deacon or a priest?

The sincere disciple of Christ can so far speak with certainty of his own spiritual experience. The accidents and the circumstances of his own experience may also at times be spoken of; they will give life and colour to what he is describing. And he will be too humble and too broad-minded to expect that the experience of others will be exactly like his own. The great principles will be traceable, but he will remember that no two lives are alike, and that God fulfils Himself in many ways. But while one can speak with confidence of what God has done for oneself in the matter of forgiveness, regeneration and perhaps renewal, one cannot speak of one's own attainment in other steps which one is bound to take, if following the Saviour—Surrender, Consecration, Sacrifice. The Bishop of Liverpool aptly summarized these steps in his sermon at the Consecration of the present

Bishops of Manchester and of Colchester on the words, "These are they which follow the Lamb whithersoever He goeth" (Revelation xiv. 4). He spoke of the call to us to follow the Saviour in the self-emptying of Bethlehem, the self-surrender of Gethsemane, the self-sacrifice of Calvary. Have we yet trodden in any of these paths? We dare not say that we have gone to Bethlehem, or to Gethsemane, or to Calvary. When we have kept back part of the price, how can we speak of our imperfect, our vitiated offering of ourselves? Still less can we, like Ananias and Sapphira, profess that we have surrendered all and say, "My all is on the altar." Of God's work in the soul, we may know and speak plainly, but of our response to God's work we can only speak with diffidence, though our wish may be to make a true and full answer to the working of His Spirit in our hearts. Such must be our growth in grace and in the knowledge of our Lord and Saviour Jesus Christ. "The one thing worth living for," said the Bishop of Truro at a Confirmation in 1900, "is likeness to Christ, and to have made that our aim will be the one thing in our lives for which we shall be thankful at the Day of Judgment." Likeness to Christ we may well

feel to be the aim and sum of all Christian
experience and effort.

Forgive me if in saying all this I have kept
you on ground well trodden and familiar. I
have not wished to confine you to the first
principles of the doctrine of Christ. But my
purpose is well illustrated by a remark of the
clergyman who prepared me for Confirmation;
" Nothing is more wonderful in Grace than the
salvation of a minister of Christ." I used to
wonder what he meant. I understand a little
now. The awful responsibility for the souls of
his people weighed upon him. The danger of
familiarity with holy things, and the fear of loss
of freshness in the work of God were ever
present to his mind. The severe temptations
which—though little suspected by others—
beset the minister of Christ did not lose their
power as years went by. And as the solemn
account came nearer and nearer, the solemnity
of his position came home to the mind of a
faithful servant. You will do well to realize all
this at the outset of your ministry. You may
be tempted to draw back, and to ask, Who is
sufficient for these things? But after all our
sufficiency is of God, and if He is putting you
into the ministry you need not be afraid to
take the step of entering it. All the way

through it we must take the position of the penitent publican and depend for acceptance with God on pardon through the precious Blood of Christ.

Whatever we are, let us aim at consistency. If our Christianity is external or superficial, consistency will be most difficult. The working of two motives—especially if opposed to one another—must produce inconsistency. But the more we know by practical experience of conversion, regeneration and renewal, following that knowledge up by consecration of ourselves to the Lord, the more practicable will consistency become. Consistency will never be easy, but it will become more possible. Aim then at being consistent, and this not so much for the sake of your people as for the sake of your credit as a Christian man and for the honour of your Master Himself. Lot's inconsistency caused his warnings to be discredited. "He seemed as one that mocked unto his sons-in-law" (Genesis xix. 14). Remembering also the need of progress in the Divine life, and the fact that we do not stand still—we either go forward or go backward—we ought to make careful use of self-examination. "Examine yourselves, whether ye be in the faith" (2 Cor. xiii. 5). Frequent self-examina-

tion may convict you of much failure, of waste
of time and opportunities, of insufficient prayer
and study of God's Word, of weak faith, of
scanty hope for heaven, of little love for the
Lord.   This may lead to improvement by
better use of the means of grace.   And conviction of shortcoming may be the foundation
of those convictions which will not perhaps in
your case build Cathedrals, but will build you
up in your most holy faith, and help you to
build living souls into the spiritual Temple
of the Lord Jesus Christ.

III.

THE FIELD AND THE FLOCK.

"THE field is the world" (St. Matthew xiii. 38). So said our Lord in the parable of the Wheat and the Tares. This imagery is equally applicable in connection with the Pastoral idea. But in another sense the field is that part of the wide world in which the few sheep committed to our charge are tended. John Wesley might say, 'The world is my parish,' but we are not John Wesleys, and we must seek a smaller field for the tending of our sheep. Yet we must beware of saying, 'My parish is my world.' A narrow parochialism is above all things to be avoided. And it is best avoided by taking an interest in other fields than our own.

The Foreign Mission-field must have a high place in our affections. Our Lord's last command ere His Ascension entrusted to His people the work of making the Gospel known to all nations and to every creature. And His Apostles made it their aim to carry the Gospel to pagan countries. St. Paul's ambition was to preach Christ where He was not already named.

For many centuries the Church of Christ had almost forgotten her first duty, but during the past century a great awakening has taken place. Many fields have been entered, and Foreign Missions are coming to be recognized as the first duty of the Church of Christ. Some of you may find your way to the Foreign Mission-field. But I would put in a plea for more than this. Let there be the deliberate facing of the question by each one, whether God is not calling you personally to the Foreign Mission-field. 'The evangelization of the world in this generation' is the bold motto of the Students' Volunteer Missionary Union, but it is not impracticable, if the question of God's will in the matter is fairly faced by every man who enters the Ministry. Even if the decision be for work in the Home Mission-field, the chief work of the Christian Church must still receive our interest, our prayers and our support. It will be our duty to rouse and to instruct our people on this subject; to elicit their prayers and gifts, and the offering of themselves in some cases for foreign service. But we shall never get them very far forward unless we love missionary work ourselves and know what is going on in the Mission-field. In some dioceses questions on modern missionary work are set in the Bishop's examinations, giving thereby a hint as to one line of study which the young clergyman should take. And nothing is more helpful than to join a younger clergy missionary union. The Church Missionary Society founded such an Union some twenty years ago, and the Society for the Propagation of the Gospel followed suit. Some thousands of the younger clergy are now numbered among their members. Most candidates for ordination receive from the secretaries an invitation to join, but failing that an application to the head office for membership will be welcomed.

Akin to Foreign Missionary work is work in the Colonies. South Africa, Canada, and Australia, not to speak of other parts of the world, present numberless openings which the decrease of candidates for Holy Orders makes it hard to fill.

The work of most of you will lie at

first in the Home Mission-field. And though its claims cannot compare with those of the Foreign Field, its problems are sufficient to cause great searchings of heart to earnest Churchmen. Look at London for instance, its six million people shared by three dioceses. The Bishop of London is never tired of telling us that his diocese of over three million souls has forty thousand added to its population every year. South London in the new Diocese of Southwark has its million and three-quarters, and is still growing—flooding the valley of the Wandle with two thousand new houses every year, and adding to Lewis-ham at so prodigious a rate that it is difficult to spiritually fulfil the old meaning of its name, 'the home of the dear Son.'[1] But neither London north of the Thames nor London south of the Thames will compare for urgency with London-over-the-Border, as Dickens named that part of London which lies beyond the River Lea. There three-quarters of a million people live in some fifty parishes, and are being reinforced by thirty thousand new inhabitants each year. There villages have to be transformed into towns and provided with all the institutions which go to make a town—

[1] See Rochester Diocesan Society's pamphlet, 1904.

Social Service

from town hall, schools and baths to water, lighting and sewers. More important still the right men have to be found to serve on public bodies in these districts, and these are not always forthcoming. Most important of all the right atmosphere has to be created in the public life of these great towns; there are no traditions or precedents to guide, and no public spirit of long existence. Here is an opportunity and a task before the Church. Yet the difficulty of the work is shewn by the fact that the average population of each parish is 14,000, and that the staff of clergy is seriously undermanned. What a calamity it will be if the Church fails to gain hold in her Master's Name of these districts of Greater London. If the Church is to keep pace with London's growth, if she is merely to hold her own with the existing population, her whole energy and resources, both clerical and lay, must be brought to bear upon the task. Some of our provincial towns tell much the same story. A northern town of vast population produced in 1903 one candidate for Confirmation in every 307 of its population, whereas the normal number of candidates should be one in 50. Many of our large towns could tell most disappointing stories, and we soon learn that the Home Mission-field presents peculiar difficulties of its own.

For each of you the field will be a compara-tively small field—one field in the midst of an enormous estate. You will, however, remember the relation of your field to the great field of which it forms a part. Your parish will never be your world.

I have been speaking hitherto of the *field*. Our attention must now be given to the *flock*. There may be some confusion of thought between the two. "Ye, my flock, the flock of my pasture, are men" (Ezekiel xxxiv. 31). And I have been taking the field in the sense of the people who inhabit the field. This confusion of ideas, if it be such, is not my own merely. The word 'world' comes to mean not only the material framework in which man's lot is cast, but the men who inhabit the world. And when we think of a place we think largely of the people who dwell there. Even a village which we visit chiefly for the natural beauty of its surround-ings would lose its charm and perhaps even become repellent, if there were no signs of human life. And we choose our parish not because of the beauty of the surroundings, the healthiness of the climate, the facilities

for intercourse with so-called society, or even
the opportunities of access to stores of learning, but for the souls to be found therein.
Our first thought is for the souls for whom
Christ died, and whom He is sending us to
shepherd.

The meaning of the word 'flock' must also
not be limited. In one sense it includes those
who are members of the Church, in another
all the population. It may mean all men—all
Christ's people—the Christians in one parish—
one particular congregation. In its wider sense
the flock includes all the people within the
official sphere of our influence. When our
Lord "saw the multitudes, He was moved
with compassion on them, because they fainted,
and were scattered abroad, as sheep having
no shepherd" (St. Matthew ix. 37).

Even in the narrow confines of an English
parish there is endless variety in the
parishioners. Many ranks and classes, many
callings and trades will be represented. People
of varying religion or denomination will be
there, and people of none at all. There
will be the ungodly, the atheistic, the agnostic,
the indifferent. There will be the Nonconformist on one hand, and the Roman Catholic
on the other. In their hundred, and perhaps

in their thousand, they are to receive your ministration. A mile or more of streets is in your own district. You are set to begin your work. You may well cry with the Psalmist, " Who will bring me into the strong city ? " (Psalm lx. 9). You may well ask, What am I among so many ? But as in the miracle of old, so now the Saviour may take you, if you put yourself and what you have into His hands, and He may break you and feed the multitude. You are willing to be used for His glory and as He will. And Henley's lines may be applied to our Church, quite as aptly—I hope—as to our country :

> "Take us and break us :
> We are yours, England, my own."

But I speak now not of the actual work which you will be doing, rather of the characteristics of the flock in general. And this is necessary, for you must understand something of men if you are really to bring home to them the message of God. Pastoral Theology you will remember consists in the application of what we know of God to the needs of men. And we must know something of the particular men to whom we are sent. We must find out what interests them, how they spend their spare time, what they do on Sundays.

F

Diocesan Conferences and Church Congresses
may discuss questions of Church Government,
but—as a Hertfordshire paper observed recently,
commenting on one such discussion, "The
supposed divine origin of any form of Church
government arouses very little interest now
among the great mass of the people compared
with the place it once filled in men's minds."
The man in the street in England is not like
his fellow in Egypt, who, if a Copt, will discuss
in the café the question of the Divine and
human nature of our Lord, or, if a Moham-
medan, will argue on the Divinity of Christ.
At the same time we may be thankful that
religious questions do arouse the greatest
interest amongst the people. Even when
the argument is against Christianity, the sale
of a book by thousands of copies is a proof
of the interest felt in the subject. The circulation of hundreds and thousands of copies of
volumes published by the Rationalist Press
Association tells its story. Read some of
these books, see what people are thinking
about. Such works as those of Robert Blatch-
ford and the late Samuel Laing deserve our
attention. And if you read *God and My
Neighbour*, do not forget that there are books
on the other side. *The Religious Doubts of*

Democracy will at least be familiar to you by name. At any rate try to understand the position of others. Some clergymen live in a fool's paradise. Their churches are full, and they imagine that nearly all the parishioners are there, and that the rest think with them. On taking up work in a former parish I suggested at a clerical meeting, as a subject for discussion, 'the local strength of scepticism.' Two clergymen stated that there was none, but the subject was accepted. Unhappily, I was selected to prepare the paper, a choice very disagreeable to myself, a stranger to the people and the town, as I had wished to profit by the experience of others. However, I made inquiries in various directions, and read my paper, giving circumstantial details without names. One of the clergymen present who had worked in the town for years was taken aback at the revelations which I made, and could hardly believe what I stated of various people whom he could identify from my descriptions. The recent correspondence in the *Daily Telegraph* on the question, "Do we believe?" has been of great service in revealing to us the minds of men. Under the disguise of anonymity many have laid bare secrets which they never would have disclosed to us, and the reasons for the unbelief of some and for the belief of others will repay study and analysis.

The condition of the people must receive our close attention. A clergyman must take an interest in social questions, if he is to minister to the flock in its wider sense. The Christian Church is intended to elevate and uplift, but she cannot do so unless the clergy give a wholesome lead. Interest in such questions as housing, education, temperance, the care of children, sweating—should engage our attention. We must remember that the revival of true religion has been followed by attention to social questions. The Evangelical Revival was followed by the movement for the abolition of slavery, under the leadership of such men as Wilberforce and Buxton. Soon after came the passing of the Factory Acts and the mitigation of many social evils, largely owing to the influence of Lord Ashley, afterwards Earl of Shaftesbury. And in earlier days still the Reformation was not without fruit in this respect. Bishop Gore, in a recent sermon on Hugh Latimer, claimed that his illustrious predecessor in the See of Worcester would have been called a Christian Socialist had he lived to-day.

Many crying needs await attention. Social sores need heeling, social evils need removal. At a farmhouse the other day I noticed a book entitled "Sheep-scab and how to cure it." The preface says "Scab is the sheepman's curse the wide world over. Everybody is agreed that it ought to be eradicated, and that its continued existence is a reproach. But how is the eradication to be accomplished? Some are in favour of compulsory dipping, believing it to be the only effective method. Others oppose this as tyrannical and wholly unnecessary. The subject is bristling with difficulties." The flock of Christ suffers from the same complaint. "From the sole of the foot even unto the head there is no soundness in it ; but wounds and bruises, and putrefying sores : they have not been closed, neither bound up, neither mollified with ointment" (Isaiah i. 6). We must understand these evils : we must desire their removal. For this it is requisite that we should know the people. And though we may not be wise enough to devise a remedy for the social ills around us, nor powerful enough to effect their cure, it will be something for the people to know that their welfare is a matter of the deepest concern to ourselves. Do not be in a hurry to arrive at an opinion on these matters, and above all, hesitate before laying the blame on parties whom you do not know to be responsible. It is not only the landlord who is responsible for high rents and overcrowded dwellings, or even summary evictions. The brewer and the publican are not solely responsible for the drunkenness which prevails in our parishes. Bishop Fraser said in 1871, " With me social questions have taken rank, not only far above political but even far above ecclesiastical questions. . . . I mean . . . that without relaxing my hold on what I believe to be the great truths of Christianity, I still feel that the great function of Christianity is to elevate man in his social condition " (Hughes' *Life of Bishop Fraser*).

Questions affecting the employment of labour will come under your notice. The conditions of employment and the want of employment will be matters of the first importance in a working-class parish. You may come into contact with trades unions, or other phases of the labour movement. And much of this will be new to you. Hitherto your surroundings have been wholly different, and you have perhaps never come into contact with this side of life. The temptation may come to you to become a thorough-going Radical, or to go

farther and join the ranks of the Labour Party,
or even to affect Socialistic views.

The tendency is very natural, but beware of
two mistakes. Much of what now comes home
to you with such force appeals to you rightly.
You ought to know these things, and to take
them to heart. But do not rush to a conclusion
without hearing and studying both sides of a
question. In differences between labour and
capital do not assume that labour is wholly in
the right, and capital wholly in the wrong.
Though your lot may not have been cast
hitherto with the sons of labour, neither has it
been cast with the masters of capital. Capital
and labour are brethren. One cannot exist
without the other. Our attitude should be—
" Sirs, why do ye wrong one to another ? "
You are not likely to frown upon the labour
movement, or to condemn it for obvious mistakes and shortcomings. Do not rush to the
other extreme. Remember that John Burns
himself knows the weaknesses of his friends,
and is not slow to tell them what they are.

Another mistake is made by some in all
sincerity. Clergymen will throw in their lot
with the labour movement in one way or
another in the laudable hope of gaining influence with working men, of doing them good,

and of bringing them to Church. They may or may not succeed. But even if the result be to bring scores of working men to Church, such a course is not justified thereby. If the labour cause is championed by the clergy, it must be because that cause is right, and because it is right for the clergyman to espouse it. Principle and not expediency must be one's guide in such matters.

The transition from this question to that of politics is natural. Politics must receive your attention, party politics may. You may, as one whose πολίτευμα is in heaven, wish well to the politics of earth. You may wish, as the inscription on Edmund Burke's statue at Bristol runs, to 'have your share of doing good and resisting evil' (Speech at Bristol, 1780). But you will be slow to identify yourself with one political party or the other, unless temporarily when some question of national righteousness is at stake. You will see so much good in both parties that you will hesitate to side with one against the other. And you will see so many good men, and so much good in men on both sides, that you will prefer backbone to colour.

Some time ago the Secretary of the Liberal Club in our parish stated to me that he wished to resign his position and to devote his spare time to work for God. I sympathized with his desire, but was anxious that the Liberals should not think that the Church had tried to detach my friend from their cause. So I asked him whether he had looked at the matter from every point of view and told him that I preferred that he should be Secretary of the Liberal Club rather than of the Conservative. He replied that he had considered the matter very carefully, and that he had safe-guarded the position of the Church amongst his political friends. The result was that we gained an excellent worker.

An objection to my advice will be at once urged: One political party is bent upon fighting the Church, robbing her of her endowments and privileges; how can we help setting ourselves against that party? Now I am keenly alive to the importance of Church Defence. I fully believe in the Establishment, I recognize the value and the usefulness of endowments and privileges. But what should be the first wish of the Church's sons? To abide by the stuff, to hold fast to it at all costs? No, certainly not. The highest interests of the people at large must be the first care of the Church and specially of the clergy. And if the support of some movement vitally affecting the nation involves danger to the national Church, we must run that risk and be ready to suffer the loss of all things that we may benefit our country. If the Church is true to the nation, I believe that the nation will be true to the Church. If not, we must remember again that sacrifice is the path of progress, and that he who loses his life shall save it. By all means take up Church Defence and Church Instruction, work in which you will derive great assistance from the Committee which bears that name. But do not let the Church become your politics. There are larger and wider issues before Churchmen than the maintenance of the existing status of a system, however 'ancient, however widespreading, and however fruitful in saints.' No action by the State can destroy the Church, and the more exalted the view we take of her character, the less risk shall we fear of her suffering harm.

At the same time do not be a party to the movement for Disestablishment which is growing within the Church. The advantages of liberation from State control may be more fancied than real. And a check to extravagant hopes has been given by the recent decision respecting the United Free Church

of Scotland.   It is one thing not to put in
the first place the retention of property and
privilege, it is another to put one's hand to
the destruction of what it has taken centuries
to build up.

In any town parish, especially if it be the
mother parish of the District, you will be
brought into contact with the civic and municipal authorities.   Direct relations with them
will be more in the hands of your Vicar than
in your own.   But you will have many opportunities of shewing and encouraging respect
to the local authorities.   Do not look down
on them, if their members are not conspicuous
for their social status or administrative ability,
or for their attendance at Church.   By all
means oppose bumbledom, and discourage
snobbery or self-interest in the taking of
municipal office; but encourage a healthy
ambition for a share in local government, and
foster readiness to enter public life for the
benefit of the community.

Avoid conflict between the civic and the
ecclesiastical bodies in a parish, and as you
have opportunity of becoming acquainted with
the members and officials of public bodies, try
to deepen in them respect for your Vicar and
to win their individual adherence to the cause

of true religion. Once a year perhaps the public authority may attend service at the parish church. Do not feel amused, still less poke fun, at the accompaniments of municipal officialism, the gowns of councillors or the mace of the mayor, but remember that the powers that be are ordained of God, and that their representatives do well to remember that they too are the ministers of God for good, attending continually upon this very thing. Much good may come of this union of Church and State in public worship. Nobler ideals, higher tone, more disinterested policy may be the outcome of what one of our local papers calls the annual 'Churching' of the District Council. It is said that a few years ago, when a question was being debated in a Committee of a certain Council, a not too laudable policy was being advocated by certain Councillors, and that the discussion was interrupted with the remark, " Mr. J—— told us when we were at church that we were *stewards*." The remark brought back to mind the text of the Vicar's previous sermon to the Council, and it is said that wiser counsels at once prevailed, a better spirit took possession of the Committee, and a right course was decided on.

I have spoken of some of the questions which

we must face if we desire to be pastors of the flock in our parish, taking the word in the wider sense which Scripture allows and our Church expects. We may look at the people from the point of view of social, or from that of moral characteristics. It is not enough to classify people as rich and poor, or even as upper classes, middle classes, and working classes. Each class has many grades with distinctions which are not merely the creation of class prejudice. The Right Honourable Charles Booth in his work on *Life and Labour in London: Religious Influences*, classifies society thus : " The five classes which we have recognised are wealth (with fashion), upper middle class (without fashion), lower middle class, regular wage earners, and the poor " (series iii. vol. v. p. 44). You will be the last to be moved by any feeling of class superiority, yet you cannot ignore these distinctions. And it would not be wise to do so. To recognize them may help to keep up a healthy sense of self-respect. Snobbishness is altogether to be blamed, but the feeling which makes a father and mother particular as to which school their children attend is not to be put in that category. There may be much effort to retain or to attain a certain social status, and where means are scanty the struggle may be severe. Surely this is worthy of all praise, if the desire be to preserve or improve the tone, manner, and bearing of the younger members of a family. Set your face against anything like airs and graces, pride, jealousy, or aping the position or manners of another class. The Church's influence should be so brought to bear on class distinctions that what is bad in them should disappear. The Church knows no class distinctions as such. All are one in Christ Jesus : all are neighbours : all are brethren.

Akin to this is the question of neighbours. One phenomenon of modern large parishes is the long streets in which many inhabitants are quite proud of not even knowing the names of their next-door neighbours. This is preferable to the intimate knowledge of the affairs of neighbours which marks some parishioners, specially in country or small town parishes. But it is not healthy, and it is fatal to any community of feeling, or to the existence of public spirit amongst the parishioners, or to the growth in every class of the sense of civic responsibility. Yet withal you will often find that the poor help one another to a wonderful degree. An overworked mother will sit up all night with a sick neighbour, or one family will give of its scanty earnings money or food to help another. Instances of heroic self-denial and of noble self-sacrifice will come under your notice from time to time.

To whatever class you may be called to minister, go as the messenger of Christ. Do not be silent to upper-class folk on the very subject of your mission ; do not force on people of the working classes what you would not dare to mention to the rich. Try to remember always that you are a witness for Christ, and you will give your message in a manner adapted to the needs of the class to which you minister. But if the thought of your mission comes only second in your own mind, you will then be pandering to the class you approach, with just a dash of religion or a mention of your message thrown in.

Looking at your parishioners from a moral and religious standpoint, you will have to cope with various influences. There are the downright ungodly, those who flaunt their vice ; those who take delight in dishonouring God and anything associated with Him—the Lord's House, the Lord's Day, and the Lord's people ; those who have no wish to interfere with anyone else so long as they are allowed to continue in sin; those who hide their vice either from fear of detection or to bear a better name than they deserve. Then there are the submerged tenth, and others for whom the battle of life has proved too much, who are without hope and without God in the world; they are lost sometimes to all sense of decency and shame, and often to all religious instinct. There are the indifferent, whether those to whom the pursuit of money or pleasure is the absorbing passion, or those who have enough to do to keep body and soul together without taking up—as they tell you—with Church and Chapel going. There are the merely secular; men without a sky, as has been said; and men who will only believe what they can touch or see. From a slightly different point of view you have to reckon with the atheistic, a small family, but one possessing numbers of cousins in the agnostics. There are the materialists and so called free-thinkers, who assume that no one who thinks can be Christian.

There are also votaries of other religions. The parish may contain hundreds or even thousands of Jews. Their number will largely determine what kind of effort you will make to reach them. If they are in your midst in multitudes you will need special methods to deal with them, such as are attempted by Mr. Davies in Spitalfields, or Mr. Poynder in Whitechapel. Take every opportunity of gaining an insight into such work. You will hardly be able to originate it yourself in any parish without careful study of the Jewish position and observation of the work of experts. If the Jews are few in number, you can approach them individually as you come across them. With the younger people you may have the better prospect of success, though you should never attract Jewish boys or girls to instruction without the consent of their parents. In some cases this will be given, and given without any thought of material advantage.

Other elements will compose the flock beside the inner circle of Church people, and these Christian elements of very differing character—Roman Catholics and Nonconformists. In regard to the former we cannot afford to ignore either the past history of the Church of Rome or the aims of her present leaders. Domination over every department of life is the great aim of the Papacy. And as her yoke proved intolerable to England in the past, so it would prove again. We must view the Roman Church in the light of its doctrines and also as a political system. We must keep clearly in our minds the additions to Scriptural doctrine which she has foisted on her adherents; the place which she accords to the Virgin Mary; her teaching of Transubstantiation; and the claims of the Papacy. At the same time the history of the Inquisition abroad and the attempts of Rome to regain ascendency after the Reformation at home, shew clearly her political aims. We have only to take the published utterances of the late Cardinal Manning and the late Cardinal Vaughan to see what is the purpose of the Church of Rome for England to-day. But while we take so serious a view of the Roman Church as a system, we shall readily distinguish between the system and its votaries.

We shall gladly extend every courtesy to the Roman Catholic priest working in our own district. We shall probably find him thoroughly earnest and sincere—though earnestness and sincerity are not necessarily criteria of truth,—and he may be given up to a life of self-denial. At times controversy with him in private or in public may be necessary, but it will be better to entrust its conduct to your Vicar. How far it is right to attempt to win Roman Catholics to a purer faith is questioned by some, but in the light of Scripture, of history, and of the conditions required by our Bishops before the admission of Roman Catholics to the Church of England, ought we to be content that they should remain as they are? In some cases even where the number of Roman Catholic parishioners is large, the Protestant population may also be sufficiently large to require the whole of our time. What may be done in such cases can be learnt from the work of the Irish Church Missions to Roman Catholics. But whatever is done, let it be straightforward and in the full light of day.

Every parish—at any rate every parish which requires an assistant curate—will have centres of one or more Nonconformist denominations, and isolated members of others. In your relations with them there will be ample opportunity for the display of tact. The injudicious action of a clergyman may go far to disturb the peace of a whole parish. Our Ordination vows speak very plainly on this point. "Will you maintain and set forwards, as much as lieth in you, quietness, peace and love, among all Christian people, and especially among them that are or shall be committed to your charge?" Thoughtful people cannot

but regret the divisions amongst Christians.
They seem contrary to the mind of Christ,
and are provocative of many practical dis-
advantages in Christian work, in connection
with the relief of the poor ; the maintenance
of spiritual discipline ; the expense of maintaining several centres for the same purpose ;
unnecessary ministration in some places, and
insufficient attention to others. Some people
talk glibly about healthy rivalry, and friendly
competition. This is mere nonsense, and
wholly alien to the Spirit of Christ. But
doubtless the fault of the existence of Nonconformist denominations is quite as much
ours as their own. History points many a
lesson here, and speaks of the witness borne
by many of these denominations to some
forgotten side of truth.

Welcome, therefore, Nonconformists who
hold fast to the Divinity of our Lord as
fellow-Christians. If they are baptized with
water into the Name of the Father, the Son,
and the Holy Ghost, they are Christians.
There can be no two opinions as to that.
And whether you feel scruples about their
Orders, or whether you believe them to be
perfectly valid, the responsibility on that score
rests on their shoulders, not on yours, and

you can legitimately receive them as coming in the name of the Lord Jesus.

Much will be gained if the world can see that we love all fellow-Christians, even though they follow not with us. Too long have Churchmen and Nonconformists been opposing one another, forgetting that there are foes of both awaiting their opportunity at their gates—foes which they will only overcome united. And there are tasks before the Church of Christ whose non-fulfilment causes grave questionings in some minds as to the savour of Christianity in the world. On many questions we can unite our forces—the liquor traffic ; the social evil ; child labour ; relation of labour to capital ; the housing problem ; immigration ; desecration of the Lord's Day ; marriage and divorce. Never sneer at the Nonconformist conscience. It has fulfilled a very useful purpose, and one fears that a Church conscience has yet to come into being as a practical force. Would that the differences arising from the education question might be put to rest, and that we might set ourselves to heal some of England's open sores. We should thus get to know one another better, and mutual understanding would help to prepare the way for that reunion of the Churches which we

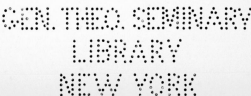

hope may one day come. You will sometimes find Nonconformists coming over to the Church, you may also find the reverse happen occasionally. If they come to you to seek admission to the Church, do not admit them without some inquiry as to their motive. It may be better that they should remain where they are, and in any case transference from one religious denomination to another is too serious to occur at the dictate of a mere whim. Where conviction prompts the step the case is wholly different. Even then let the procedure be straightforward, and bid your new adherent apprise his minister of the step which he proposes to take.

There remain to be considered those who are your flock in the inner sense of the word. Our Lord said, "I am the Good Shepherd, and know My sheep, and am known of Mine" (St. John x. 14). This must be the aim of the pastor, but in most town parishes and in many country parishes it is impossible to achieve. We must not on that account confine our attention to a faithful few. The flock in its widest sense demands our attention, and must have it in the various directions which I have described. We must in some sort of way aim at reaching all our parishioners.

But our own people must be our special care.
We must know and love them with an intensity
which is impossible in the case of a wider
circle. We must permit them to know us
more intimately than would be possible for
two or three thousand parishioners.

Such intimacy implies accessibility on our
part. Often at unwelcome times we must welcome callers; we must be ready to give them
time and thought; we must allow them to know
us as we really are. In some parishes too
much attention is lavished on a comparatively
small circle. The same people come to the
different services; the same attend the different
meetings; the same are members of the various
societies and guilds. In such a parish the
influence of the Church will be stationary,
and while beloved by a few the clergy
will probably be unknown even by sight to
half the parishioners. Our aim should be
like that of our Lord, to train some to
influence others in their turn. Try to estab-
lish a centre of work, however humble, in
every corner of the parish. Try to plant a
Christian home, or at least one communicant
in every street, and let none be content with
merely receiving the ministrations of the
Church. Let each be given some definite

work to do, and be taught to aim at influencing others. Prepare your people to endure
hardness, as good soldiers of Jesus Christ.
Teach them that Christians ought to set an
example to the world, to be ready to stand
alone, and to be leaders in their own surroundings. You must be ready to cheer in moments
of discouragement. "Fear not, little flock, for
it is your Father's good pleasure to give you
the Kingdom" (St. Luke xii. 32). Keep your
people together, teach them to preserve the
unity of the Spirit in the bond of peace. And
do not view with complacency the alienation of
any Church people from their parish church.
I have heard of clergymen who have even
boasted of having cleared out an old congregation and of having put a new one in its place.
Others seem strangely indifferent to the alienation of worshippers of long standing owing
to innovations or alterations which arouse
their prejudices or wound their consciences.
Neither attitude is to be recommended for
imitation.

Do not aim at popularity with, or even
the affection of your inner circle. Think ever
of what is best for their welfare, and be content at times to be misunderstood. Do not
make them lean too much on yourself, but

cause them more and more to lean directly
on Christ, and to draw their support from
Him.   Develop in them spiritual backbone.
Train them to know why they are Christians
and why they are Churchmen, and to be able
to tell other people their reasons.   Teach them
to act upon definite principles based on loyalty
to their Divine Master.   Then consistency will
become more attainable and respect from the
world will be won the better.

Feed and tend the sheep and the lambs of
Christ's flock.   See that you have food to give
them.   In many a parish "the hungry sheep
look up and are not fed."   And if in your parish
some shortcoming seems to mark the character
or work of your people, ask yourself whether
the fault may not be laid at your own door.

In the days of my training for the Ministry
the Principal of our College occasionally had to
find some fault with the men.   With characteristic humility he always first laid the blame
on himself, though entirely undeservedly.   This
made us love him all the more.   And if with
more reason you lay the blame of the failings of your people upon yourselves, or at
least admit a share of the responsibility, you
will not lose their affection, and they will
walk with you further on the road to God.

IV.

THE FOLD.

The imagery of the Shepherd and his Flock is not complete without a picture of the Fold. There must be some place where the sheep can be sheltered, protected and cared for, and in England at any rate—fed and watered. Out in the East conditions are somewhat different. The fold is often of a permanent character. Substantial walls built of stone enclose a resting place for the sheep, where weary after their day's journeying at the call of the shepherd to obtain pasture and water, they enter by the one door in the evening, and rest secure from fear of molestation by their foes. In England the fold serves a more temporary purpose. It is constructed of hurdles as a rule, and the shepherd moves it to fresh pasture as occasion may demand. For the purposes of this lecture each fold has its counterpart. The permanent sheepfold in the East we may compare to the Church of England. The form of fold common in this country we may compare to the parishes where souls are shepherded from time to time, and in particular to the parish church, which is the centre of parochial life, worship and work.

Of the clergyman in relation to the Church of England as a whole, and to his parish church in particular I wish next to speak.

In one sense the flock of Christ is only one —"I believe one Catholic and Apostolic Church," but the folds of Christ are many. We have drifted into thinking of the fold as if it were one. And perhaps this mistake is due largely to the mistranslation of St. John x. 16 in the Authorised Version—"Other sheep I have, which are not of this fold : them also I must bring, and they shall hear My voice ; and there shall be one fold, and one Shepherd." The word 'fold' in the last clause should read 'flock'—"one flock and one Shepherd." On this Bishop Westcott observes, "The translation 'fold' for 'flock' has been most disastrous in idea and in influence" (*Commentary on St. John*, note on ch. x. 16). "It would perhaps be impossible for any correction now to do away with the effects which a translation undeniably false has produced on popular ecclesiastical ideas " (additional note on St. John x. 16). Disaster has certainly followed the attempt to set up one fold for the whole world, but in spite of this Rome still prefers her claims. And we must recognize the fact that even in England we cannot drive all Christians into one fold. The flock may be one, but the folds many. This may seem to run counter to dearly cherished beliefs as to the visible unity of the Catholic Church. But experience in the Christian Ministry soon teaches one that it is of no use to try to square facts to fit our theories. We must adapt our theories to the facts. And to know that Scripture recognizes the existence of more than one fold will save us from serious misgiving.

Men often speak of the Holy Catholic Church as consisting of three main branches, the Roman, the Greek and the Anglican, but those three branches are not one. They have many links, it is true, but they are divided each against one another. The folds are many, though all may contain members of the one flock of Christ.

Look at the matter in another light. Some

tell us that the Church of England is the Branch of the Holy Catholic Church in this land. Baptism admits to the Holy Catholic Church. Many people are validly baptized who are not members of the Church of England. Therefore the Church of England is not entirely conterminous with the Holy Catholic Church in England. Recollection of this fact will prevent us from acting in an arbitrary manner, or from expecting to force the Christians of England into one fold. Nor shall we wish to abolish, or even to depreciate other folds, however irregular their construction may be. But for all that the Church of England will be for us the fold in this country, and where we cannot drive we shall be glad to lead. The shepherd "goeth before them, and the sheep follow him : for they know his voice" (St. John x. 4).

No one theory quite meets the whole case. It is enough for us to obtain a working theory, and then to give ourselves to the work of the Ministry.

There are multitudes who look upon the Church of England as their fold, and to whom our ministrations will be acceptable. And we can seek for those who are outside any fold. There are many thousands who answer this description. It has been remarked that Nonconformist denominations suffer very few of their adherents to sink so low as the workhouse. The reply has been made that if the large majority of inmates in poor-law institutions describe themselves as members of the Church of England, they naturally turn to that Church as caring for the outcast and the fallen, to whom her Master specially appealed. We must love our fold, reverence and be proud of it, but we must remember that it is not the flock. The shepherd is to love the fold much, but the flock more. He is to love the fold as the home of the sheep, but men are to be more to him than the system which enfolds them.

We must grasp clearly the position of the Church of England at the present day.

The following facts present themselves to our minds :

(1) The Church of England is the original representative of Christianity in this country.

That is of importance in view of the divisions amongst Christians. These divisions have deplorable results, not the least of which is the perplexity which they cause to many as to which body of Christians has the strongest claim on their adherence. If we can shew that the Church of England is the representative of the earliest British Church, we go far towards establishing her Divine mission and her claim on English Christians. The origin of the British Church is lost in obscurity. It began long before the mission of St. Augustine. It may have sprung from the work of Christians who found their way to this country for purposes of commerce, government or military service. Possibly St. Paul himself may have preached in this island. In any case at a very early date we find traces of a British Church and its Bishops. And the Church of England is the direct lineal descendant of the early British Church. The historic continuity of the Church of England is a fact, and gives it a claim on the allegiance of all English Christians.

(2) The Church of England is Scriptural.

The New Testament is the manual of original Christianity. It alone contains what can be known of the life, the work and the teaching of the Lord Jesus Christ. Isolated Logia may come to light at different times and claim to be sayings of Christ. But we can only test them when on other grounds their authenticity seems undisputed, by comparing them with our Lord's sayings as recorded in the Gospels and the Acts. And the New Testament alone contains an account of the teaching and work of those who were best qualified to interpret the mind of Christ and to carry on His work—the Apostles. The greater the likeness to our Lord in the character of Church or Christian, and the closer the correspondence of their belief or teaching with His own, the more power may Church or Christian expect to have in drawing others to Christ. And with the desire to be strictly loyal to her Master the Church of England in her sixth Article limits her appeal in matters of faith to the contents of or deductions from Holy Scripture. With this view she demands of her clergy that they shall make a special study of the Scriptures. And to mark the exposition of Scripture and the preaching of the Gospel as the chief work of her ministers she now places a copy of the New Testament in the hands of her Deacons, and a copy of the whole Bible in the hands of her Priests at their ordination.

No church exactly conforms in every particular to the Church of the Apostolic age as described in the New Testament. But we may safely claim that no Church in our own land approaches more nearly to the New

Testament ideal, and that therefore in the fold of the Church of England the sheep of Christ's flock in this country may fitly find their home.

This position has not been reached without a struggle. The very best of things tend in this world of corruption to deteriorate. And the Church of Christ is ever subject to a centrifugal force, which would have it fly off at a tangent from that orbit of which Christ is the centre. At times the development of doctrine has been in wrong directions. Burdens have been laid on men's shoulders which our Lord never prescribed. Superstitions due to the influence of pagan surroundings have crept in. Abuses of various kinds have sprung up. When the time was ripe, this deterioration has been discovered, and the movement for reform has begun. In our own Church the climax was reached when the accretions of mediaevalism became intolerable. With the fuller light of increased knowledge they were thrown off at the Reformation. We have then to remember that

(3) The Church of England is Reformed.

It cannot be questioned that the Church needed reformation and that reformation did take place. The reform effected not only

H

removed abuses, but touched matters of organization and principles of doctrine and worship. Its height was reached in the Second Prayer Book of Edward VI., and though the life of that book was but short, so impartial a judge as Canon Mason tells us that our present Prayer Book takes the Prayer Book of 1552 as its model.[1] It is to be regretted that in some quarters the extraordinary blessings which the Reformation brought to Church and State in England are not sufficiently understood at the present day. We are sometimes told that the Church is not to be bound by the dead hand of the sixteenth century. This would seem to indicate a desire to bring the Church up to the date of the twentieth century, but the real source of the plea seems strangely enough to be a desire to go back to the fifteenth or fourteenth century, still further removed from the life of to-day. Our friends forget that if we shake off what they consider the fetters which bind us, by reason of their age, we may be called upon with some show of reason to surrender the still more ancient charters of our rights and liberties.

It is yours to be loyal to the Church of

---

[1] See Canon Mason's *Life of Cranmer*, page 146. (Methuen's *Leaders of Religion*.)

England in letter and in spirit. You may wish things to be different from what they are, but you are not obliged to enter her ministry. If you seek the office of a Deacon or a Priest in her service, you will naturally be expected to subject yourself to her discipline and to be true to the instructions which she gives you. Personal preferences must be put aside, and after all if any of her requirements are wrong the responsibility for their existence rests not on yourself, but on the Church which exacts them.

That Church is well suited to be the fold of the English people. The errors of Rome and the abuses of mediaevalism she has avoided. She has kept close enough to the constitution of the early Christian Church to retain her Catholic character. And by combining with a supreme respect for the Scriptures a regard for primitive antiquity, she has embodied the virtues of Puritanism without falling a victim to its failings. She accords to her clergy and still more to her laity a large measure of liberty; and though she says in effect: "This is the way, walk ye in it," she allows some limits of deviation within which those who do not like the footpath may walk upon the grass.

While the Church of England is intended to be the fold of the English people in general, you will be concerned with its presentation to a small section of the nation. And that presentation you will make chiefly by means of a Parish, a Parish Church, and the Prayer Book. The parish with its church will be the fold in which the sheep committed to your charge will be shepherded so long as they live within its bounds.

The parish will be for you the sphere, though not altogether the limit, of your parochial activities. As regards the particular parish in which you will work and your conduct in that parish towards different classes of parishioners I hope to speak in a later lecture. But I touch now the general question of the parish. Learn its exact boundaries. Read up so far as possible its past history. Find out the occupation of the people and their general character. Become conversant with the details of local administration and government. Make the acquaintance of those who are at the head of other denominations in the parish, and be on friendly terms with them. Seek an entry into the various schools in the parish; make friends with teachers and children. Take an interest —and shew it—in local movements of a beneficent character. In a word, do all you can to understand and to be understood by the people whom you hope to gather within the fold.

The Parish Church will be the local fold in its concrete form. Let that be not only the centre towards which all your parochial work will converge, but a centre of your own affection also. It may be a church of exquisite proportions or hallowed by centuries of worship, a Beverley Minster or a Malmesbury Abbey. You may be called to a church fair or large, to a St. Mary Redcliffe or to a St. Nicholas, Great Yarmouth. Or you may go to a modern church of noble design, to a St. Giles', Camberwell, or a St. Mary's, Portsea. In such cases the very building will evoke your affection and teach you its lessons.

On the other hand, your lot may be cast in a parish whose church is a bye-word for ugliness or dinginess—one of the monstrosities of eighty years ago. Its ugliness may be beyond cure. And the building may be altogether unsuited to modern ideas of worship. Do not on that account despise the building. It is hallowed by the presence of the Lord and by the worship of His people. There will be something to love in the plainest building if we have met God there and have been taught of Him. The late Mr. Newland in his lectures on

Tractarianism, advised that every opportunity should in that case be taken of pointing out to the parishioners the demerits of the fabric, and if possible its structural insecurity. Such a course has before now been taken. But it is hardly to be commended, and it seems to savour somewhat of the disingenuous. By all means make churches as beautiful as possible, but at a time when money is so much needed for new churches in overgrown districts, it seems of doubtful wisdom to pull down a church whose day is not done, unless some special gift makes possible the erection of a new one. Lack of beauty may not be open to remedy, but dinginess and other defects can be overcome. And though the initiation of, or at least the consent to improvements must rest with the Vicar, remember that a Curate can do much towards carrying them out. He will not try to force the hand of an unwilling Vicar, but he will be glad to relieve his shoulders of a burden.

I have in my mind the example of a Curate who raised some seven hundred pounds for a new organ, which was much needed in a church, but for which the Vicar was too much occupied to collect funds. One of my present colleagues has raised nearly a thousand pounds for a new mission church in his district.

In any case try to increase the respect of the people for the church. If they set little store by it, they will set little store by the Church of England and perhaps by religion itself. And remember that the Church does not belong to you, or to the Vicar, but to the people.

In some parishes the squire seems to clear the people from the parish for the sake of his pheasants, and the parson to drive them from the church for the sake of his fancies. The fold is intended for the safety and comfort of the flock, and not as a preserve of the shepherds. You at least are only likely to serve there for a few years, before being appointed to a benefice or proceeding to the Mission-field. Many of your people spend their whole lives beneath the shadow of the church, as their ancestors have done before them. Be chary then of altering custom or usage which have obtained there for many years past, unless such have been absolutely illegal or grievously offend your own conscience.

Changes in minor matters are sometimes made in churches, and members of the congregation who deplore them are told that the matter is not essential, and that they ought therefore not to feel aggrieved. But if the matter be not essential, the change need never have been made, and the clergyman had better sacrifice his own preference rather than the comfort of some of his people. In such matters you will not at first have the right of decision, but you will have opportunities of influencing your Vicar and of conciliating your people or the reverse— opportunities for shewing sympathy even with those from whom you differ.

Your concern will lie not only with the parish church as the fold into which you will aim at bringing most of your parishioners, but also with the Book of Common Prayer. You will be expected to serve as a Deacon for at least one year "to the intent you may be perfect, and well expert in the things appertaining to the Ecclesiastical Administration." It is your duty to know your Prayer Book before your Ordination as Deacon; and to know how to carry out the ritual prescribed by the Prayer Book before your Ordination as Priest. The history of the various parts of your Prayer Book ought to be your study now. You ought to be able to point out the source—ancient or modern—of any part of the Prayer Book. Our debt to the Sacramentaries of Gelasius and Gregory on the one hand, and to the revisers at the time of the Savoy Conference on the other, ought to be clear to your own mind. You ought to know what we owe to the Use of Sarum and what to the Protestantism of Strasbourg or Cologne.

When you arrive at the church where you are first appointed to serve, you ought not to need reminding as to the days for which Proper Psalms are appointed, or on which the Athanasian Creed is to be said. Even if you cannot go through the lists of these from memory, you ought to have a fairly accurate knowledge, and to entertain a shrewd suspicion as to likely days. Failing that, exercise sufficient forethought to look out before service what possible variations from the usual course may occur in the services of any particular day. Do not burden your Vicar with the necessity of telling you before the service what you are supposed to know or to find out for yourself. Nor should you spoil his worship by causing him anxiety as to whether you will give out the right Psalm or say the right Collect when you are reading Morning or Evening Prayer.

Forgive a word in particular on the subject

of reading the Banns. A glance at the rubric before the Marriage Service will save you from the frequent grammatical enormity of " *These* are *for* the first time of asking," and will remind you to announce the time of asking after the warning as to 'cause, or just impediment,' when only one set of banns is being called.

Do not wish to curtail the services unnecessarily. On one occasion at a week-day service a colleague of my own suggested that the prayers for the Royal Family might be omitted that evening. I replied, "No! an attempt might be made on the life of the Queen." The next morning the papers reported that the Prince of Wales had been shot at on that very evening in Belgium.

Avoid slovenliness of tone, manner or demeanour. Take trouble over the details of public worship. Give here of your very best to the service of God. And remember that slovenliness is no more the monopoly than it is the mark of one party in the Church. Decency and order lie just as much in simplicity of ritual as in elaborate appeal to eye, ear and even nose.

In details of ritual you will be loyal to your Vicar, neither going beyond nor falling short of his particular usage. This is your only course. But it does not relieve you of responsibility for your own usage. You may avoid accepting a Curacy at a church where the law is broken or where the Bishop is disobeyed. Wear a surplice which is neither too long nor too short. Do not wear a cassock which trails on the ground nor a hood which falls scarcely below the shoulders. Avoid crouching, stooping or lounging either when kneeling or standing. Stand up straight, with head and shoulders erect. Your very attitude may preach its own sermon. Be very particular about the neatness of your appearance in church : always let your hair be well brushed, and let your face and hands and shirt-cuffs be scrupulously clean, especially when assisting in ministering the Holy Communion. Even the shoes, or the boots, which you wear should be tidy and well shaped. It may seem superfluous to mention these little matters, but they have their own importance. Your aim should be that your person should neither attract nor distract the attention of worshippers.

Take great pains in the modulation of your voice. Be perfectly natural and at your ease. You are more likely to speak in too high a key than too low, or to speak in too loud a tone than too soft, but avoid either extreme. Excellent opportunities are given you here of receiving some training in voice production and elocution before your ordination; make every use you can of these advantages. In taking part in Divine Service beware of an unfeeling monotone, or of reading at an irreverent rate. 'A loud voice' in Prayer Book language may not mean a shout, but it does not mean a whisper. As regards demeanour, be careful at all times, when the church is empty as much as when it is full. Pay obvious and sincere attention to the sermon, when you are a listener. Even if you are tired, as you often may be with good reason, do not appear so. Nothing is more depressing in church, I have heard it said, than a jaded clergyman. Even if not musical, take your share—though no more than that—in the singing. But if you sit with the choir, be careful not to meddle in matters which are too great for you, nor to cause inconvenience to them by joining *ex tempore* in an anthem over which the choir has spent days or even weeks in preparation. To be too lusty in singing a hymn may cause amusement or annoyance to the congregation. If it falls to your lot to give out the notices do not stretch too far the latitude allowed in the rubric in the Communion office, nor include all sorts of minor parochial engagements which have no possible interest for nine-tenths of your congregation. In such a case it is best to ask your Vicar to draw up a list each week of the engagements to be announced in church, though in most well-ordered parishes you will find this done already.

In assisting at the Holy Communion be content with the directions of the Prayer Book, enriching them where they are incomplete by sanctified common sense, and not from manuals of doubtful authority. You will have your own ideas as to the right method of administering the Lord's Supper, but subordinate these to the plain meaning of the rubrics. Do not lend countenance to any attempt to reproduce the Romish Mass in our own Church. Remember the opinion of Bishop Creighton—himself no partisan—that the Reformation saw the Mass turned into a Communion (*Life and Letters*, vol. ii. ch. xiii. p. 426). Be careful never to separate even in thought the celebration of the mystery from the communion of the faithful : still less to approve its isolation in practice. Remember that the Sacrament is only complete in the reception of the sacred elements by the communicants. It is over the doctrine and ritual connected with this rite that many ecclesiastical controversies have raged and do rage. We may regard these controversies of vital importance as affecting root principles of the Christian faith, or of trivial character in view of the great truths which unite and the grave problems which beset both sides. But whatever views you take concerning them, beware of the danger of spiritual priggishness or of personal bitterness. When once the *odium theologicum* takes hold of one—alas that such an expression should have become proverbial—danger confronts the soul. Or if one is moved to look down on the teaching or practices of others, to scorn them or to despise them or their exponents, temptation faces him. The words of Christ may have an application here : " Take heed that ye despise not one of these little ones " (St. Matthew xviii. 10). This is strictly compatible with tenacious adhesion to what one believes to be right. There may be more than adhesion, the time may come when it is necessary to speak what one believes to be the truth, but the note of love must dominate the whole. ' Speaking the truth in love ' we shall best grow up unto Him who is the Head in all things. We must be willing also to receive new light—to welcome it if it comes from an unexpected quarter, or if it shines in an unexpected direction, for we are seekers after truth, and in the quest are followers of Him who is the Truth.

We have to recognize some latitude in regard to what is allowed in the Church of England. But the existence of this latitude is a strong reason for observing its limits. If excessive strictness as to detail were demanded, every man would become a law to himself. On some points the meaning of the directions in the Prayer Book is perfectly clear : here only obedience is our due. But on some points the Prayer Book does not speak so plainly ; on others our duty is not stated ; on others again it is left quite open. There latitude is allowed within certain limits. And even in certain matters which seem obvious enough to some minds, but not to others, some liberty is extended. Private usage has sprung up in many details. Usage has obtained the recognition of law. And supporters of such usage have sought at times to read their usage into the Prayer Book, and have cast reflection on those who have adhered to the older practice. And we must bear in mind that in some cases where latitude is allowed, one line of usage may be that laid down in the Prayer Book, though another line may be just within the law. We must not put both on the same level. We must aim—not at doing what we are merely not forbidden to do, still less at doing what is forbidden, but at complying with the letter and spirit of rubrics and directions.

Some details may be allowed by law which are repugnant to our own consciences. So long as they are not forced upon ourselves, we must accept the situation, and give a generous recognition to the conduct of our brethren, who within the limits of the law take advantage of the liberty accorded to them. It is open to us to attempt to get the law on certain points altered either in the direction of greater elasticity or less, provided that our conduct does not compromise the principles to which we have sworn or promised adherence. While you take a permissible line, hesitate even in your mind to condemn the perhaps more correct course adopted by others. The researches of Mr. Dearmer [1] have shewn that some details of ceremonial which are fashionable are meaningless and unauthorized, and that others which

[1] See the *Parson's Handbook*.

are the reverse have considerable historical warrant for their observance.

Forgive a reference to some vexed questions connected with the Holy Communion. The Prayer Book leaves certain matters entirely open. Take for instance Fasting Communion and Evening Communion. The Prayer Book provides for neither, and condemns neither. But I have known adherents of the one condemn the observance of the other, though my experience has been that the advocates of Fasting Communion have been less generous in this matter than the advocates of Evening Communion. Surely the right course in such a matter is to affect what one thinks most honouring to our Lord and most helpful to one's own spiritual life, and to allow the same liberty to those whose experience leads to another conclusion. By an extension of early Celebrations—a practice which is perhaps more outside the Prayer Book than that of Evening Communion—I have incurred the charge from certain quarters of giving an opportunity to adherents of Fasting Communion to carry their views into effect. Why should they not do so? Did not our Lord and the Apostles fast? Let them fast. Give every facility to them to do so. But why seek to

curtail liberty in the other direction? In
this matter we generally find criticism and con
demnation proceeding from those who have had
no experience of the practice. Evening Com
munion is criticized for the lack of historica
support; for making it impossible to communi
cate fasting; and for pandering to irreverence
But as regards historical support, it is enough
to know that the original institution took place
in the evening, and that the Prayer Book'
chief name for the rite is the Supper of the
Lord. As regards the difficulty of communi
cating fasting, there is absolutely no rule to
the effect that the Sacrament must be re
ceived fasting, in the Articles or the Prayer
Book. As regards the charge of irrever
ence, twenty years' observation and experience
of Evening Communion have failed to shew
me a single instance. The worship of the
day has prepared the communicant for the
Lord's Supper. The quiet of the evening
ministers to devotion. Work done for God
during the day can be brought to Him: the
defects of work and worker are pardoned
through the precious blood of Jesus Christ
and the worker is sent on his way with
comfort and peace. The late hour at which
at least in town parishes, the service con

cludes prevents the close of the Lord's Day from being spent in frivolity and jesting. Even if your mind is strongly set against Evening Communion, do not be hasty to condemn it.

I have spoken freely on this subject, but certainly not with a view to accentuate any differences. It would, however, be folly to minimize them. The Sacrament of the Body and Blood of Christ was meant to be a bond of union between all Christians. Unhappily, through the fault not of the Founder of our religion but of His disciples, this Sacrament has become an occasion of division. These differences may grow more acute or less. And you will have your share of influence in aggravating or healing them. Perhaps what I have said may help some to take a more charitable view of the practice of others, and to allow the spirit of love to absorb the spirit of prejudice and intolerance. In either case let our wish be the language of the hymn :

"Draw me nearer, nearer, nearer, Blessed Lord,
   To Thy precious Bleeding Side."

And if we are drawn nearer to Him, we shall be drawn nearer to one another.

The other Sacrament now demands our consideration. Perhaps as the initial rite of the

Christian Church it ought to have received our attention before Holy Communion. And certainly there is a tendency in act to clothe the second Sacrament with every kind of honour, but to relegate the former to a position of obscurity and comparative insignificance. We are apt on our notice-boards, in our almanacks and our parish magazines to give prominence to the Holy Communion, but to class Baptism with the Churching of Women. 'Churchings and Baptisms,' we often read. By the way, ought we to speak of Baptisms at all in such connection? Is not the singular number correct in such a case? By all means let the observance of Churching continue, but at the same time give Baptism its proper place. Head your announcement with 'Administration of the Sacraments,' then give particulars concerning the Administration of Baptism, then concerning Holy Communion. If possible, Baptism ought to be administered at least occasionally in the course of Morning and Evening Prayer, after the Second Lesson. Insist on the requirements of the Prayer Book as to due notice being given. It will be well to print forms for the parents to fill in and to hand in when giving notice. Insist on the sponsors, or at least two of them, being present at the service.

Much harm has been done by indiscriminate baptism of all comers. Attention has been directed to this subject of late years, and considerable discussion of it has taken place in the columns of the *Guardian* and other journals. All will agree that the Church only admits to Public Baptism on the profession of repentance and faith, either personally, or—in the case of an infant—through sponsors. To baptize without sponsors is logically to go far towards admitting the condemned practice of indiscriminately baptizing the children of heathen parents. And to baptize with sponsors who merely take a parochial rather than a personal responsibility is hardly adequate. One evening a mother walked into church and asked me to baptize her child, number seven of that ilk. On the occasion for which notice had been given the weather had prevented her from bringing the child, so she had come alone on the spur of the moment. The father was stated to be unwilling to come at any time, and there was some uncertainty as to the second Godmother (the mother being one). As the woman's home was close to the church, I postponed the Baptism till the sponsors should attend. The mother was very wrathful, and argued that in " St. Augustine's parish the Sisters used to come round and fetch my children to church, and have them done, and stand for them themselves." Whatever the truth may have been, the Sacrament had been cheapened in the mother's eyes, and it had been reduced to the level of a mechanical rite. The loss to the child in such a case may be adduced, but if after full instruction parents do not bring their child to Baptism, the responsibility rests on them, and not on the clergyman.

In all cases the Baptism of a parishioner should be preceded or followed by a visit to the home. Advantage can then be taken to explain to the parents and sponsors the nature of the obligations undertaken and the privileges received. It is well to precede the service with an interval for silent prayer, in announcing which you will ask the congregation to join in prayer for the persons to be baptized. Be careful to put the preliminary question and to see that the sponsors understand that private Baptism is as valid as public, though needing to be followed by public Admission to the Church. Remember also to pour the water into the font at the outset of the service. It is well to give an illuminated card to the sponsors with the details from the register as a memento of this service.

The Baptism of adults is a service of peculiar happiness. It will, however, perhaps not fall to you until after you are ordained Priest, while the Public Baptism of Infants may often be your duty. But be careful in pastoral visitation to trace any unbaptized persons, and to put Baptism before them as a privilege to be sought diligently if they have any desire to follow Christ. Do not deter any adult parishioners who desire to be baptized by immersion, if you find their reasons are well founded. London clergy can avail themselves of the font-grave at Lambeth, and I can speak from grateful experience of the willingness of Dr. Walpole to meet such needs.

If you are rarely called upon during your Diaconate to baptize, you will be more rarely called on to solemnize Marriages. But in view of the possibility arising, be careful by attending in your robes at such a service at an early date after your ordination to learn exactly what to do when you come to officiate. The homes of persons in your district whose banns are called should be visited prior to the marriage, if not by the Vicar, by yourself. And opportunity should be taken to find out with tact the address at which the newly married couple propose to reside, and if need be to commend them to the vicar of that parish. Speak to them a word as to the duty of serving God and of attending public worship together every week.[1]

Whether there be a burial ground attached to your church or not, you will be called upon —perhaps often—to officiate at the Burial of the Dead. When the actual burial takes place at a cemetery, the former part of the service may be said in the parish church. Here, if at any service, the utmost sympathy and consideration are called for. Do not hurry over the service. It is painful to hear the Lesson gabbled through on such occasions. Once when I sat in the vestry at a cemetery, waiting to officiate at a burial, I overheard a clergyman who was officiating in the chapel read hurriedly the opening and closing verses of the Lesson, all the intervening portion being omitted. How much more calculated to lead to God was the conduct of another clergyman in the same cemetery, who said at the graveside to a parishioner of mine who had just lost his wife : " I know what your trouble is; I have been through

[1] I have been reminded to call attention to the importance of becoming acquainted with the law of marriage, English and foreign, especially in view of the increase in the number of marriages with foreigners. A Parliamentary Blue-book gives an useful summary of foreign law on this subject.

it myself." Take heed to your words and deeds on such occasions. Do not say more than is necessary—and that in the lowest tones—to sexton or undertaker during your progress from the church to the grave. Here at any rate there is sympathy in silence. Occasionally you may discern the opportunity of saying a few solemn words to the mourners as they stand beside the grave. In any case a word or two to the chief mourners individually as they return to their carriages or pass from the churchyard may be as a seed which will bring forth fruit to life eternal. Do not let yourself become dulled or hardened by continual contact with the death or burial of your parishioners. To keep the heart tender is as important as it is to keep it young.

In the event of your officiating at Baptism, a Marriage or a Burial, you will be called on to make an entry in the parish register. Let your entries be made with the utmost care and neatness. Write in straight lines and not diagonally across the space. In making an entry in the marriage register follow exactly the directions given at the beginning of the book, even to writing the date in words rather than figures, and in giving the exact age and occupation, if any, of the bride. Fill in every detail for which space is provided, and when you have finished put the register carefully away. Take your share in treasuring and protecting registers of any antiquity, and take pains to be accurate, specially as to the entry of the year, when you are copying a certificate from a register of years gone by.

These details may seem trivial, but attention to detail is of great importance in a clergyman, and such attention will help you to become expert in the ecclesiastical administration, and ready soon to enter the office of a Priest and perhaps the better prepared at a later date to fulfil the duties of that office in a parish of your own.

So you will come to love the fold more and more, to love it not for its own sake, but for its people's and for its Owner's. And in loving the fold yourself, you will cause your people to love it too. They will feel an interest and a pride in their parish church, the fold in which they are shepherded for the time being. And in course of time their ideas will be enlarged, and they will feel a true and spiritual affection for their larger and more permanent fold, the Church of England as a whole.

V.

THE PASTOR IN THE PARISH.

SOME incidents of your ordination will stand out in your memory for life. Never shall I forget the words of the present Archbishop of Canterbury to the candidates at my ordination as Priest: "You are going most of you to very wearing work, and I thank God for it." Certainly the work of the Ministry was never more arduous than to-day. This is due partly to the higher standard of duty entertained by the clergy; partly to the failure of the laity to take their proper share in Church work; partly to the increased demands made upon them by Church people and parishioners in these exacting days; partly to the social service which the civil community expects from the clergy; and partly to the growth of population.

Much of what is expected of the clergy is

unfair and uncalled for, as Prayer and the Ministry of the Word and Sacraments are their special functions. And though no gifts or accomplishments will be without use in the work of a clergyman, the varied nature of the requirements and demands of the age make it increasingly difficult to fill the office. And while in versatility and general ability the average modern clergyman probably excels his predecessors, it is to be feared that there is a distinct decline in the preaching and the spiritual power of the present generation of clergy. In any case the exigencies of modern life make our work difficult, except in some country parishes where the work is little and the pay less.

There is, however, often a disposition to disparage country work. But many rural parishes require special pastoral gifts, and in many country parishes the influence of the Church of England is weak. Yet numbers of our best people in London parishes come up from the country. And there one has special opportunities for study and for communion with God, while the atmosphere and surroundings of country life suggest and illuminate many of the lessons of pastoral work. You must not suppose that in most country

parishes there is little to do.   A scanty population may also be sparse, and it may require miles
of travelling and hours of work to minister
to a mere handful of people.   At any rate if
you go to country parishes, you will probably
have plenty to do, for economy forbids the
employment of an Assistant Curate unless there
is work to occupy his time.

The choice of a parish for your first Curacy
lies largely with yourself.   An appointment to
a Curacy differs in this respect from the appointment to a Benefice.   And, by the way, make up
your mind never to apply directly or indirectly
for the incumbency of a parish, unless reasons
of health necessitate your seeking a lighter
charge.   I do not say so because applications
for livings generally go into the waste-paper
basket, but because of the possible consequences to yourself.   It will probably become
known in the parish that you applied for the
living, and you will be regarded as incurring an
obligation to the patrons and parish in entering
the charge.   It will also make it impossible for
you to look upon the work as a call from God,
yet without such call you have no right to
undertake it.   And if you find yourself in difficulties in your parochial work, you will be
haunted by the thought that you took the work

voluntarily on your own shoulders, and that the difficulties are of your own making. If, however, you take up work at the invitation of others and at the call of God, you will be able to fortify yourself with the assurance that He who has sent you to the parish will give you grace to meet its difficulties. Application then for an incumbency does not stand well in relation to Divine vocation, and will certainly cause disappointment after a time. At the same time you must choose your first Curacy. No choice of a Curacy is more important, because so much depends on the parish which you will enter, and the Vicar with whom you will work ; yet no choice is more difficult, as you have not yet the experience which enables you to judge rightly the conditions which make a parish the right one for the beginning of your career. For the sake of mere personal comfort too your choice is important, as you will be bound to the parish for two years, and it is well to remain in a first Curacy even longer, while discomfort will be apt to breed that spirit of unsettlement and restlessness which will not only be detrimental to spiritual life, but fatal to effective and lasting influence. In your choice it will be well to obtain the consent of your own parents where possible, and to ask the counsel of some who know you and who are in a position to judge of the respective merits of various openings.

You will choose between town and country work ; if the former is your preference, between London and provincial work.   You will choose between an upper class, a middle class, a working class, and a poor or even a very poor parish.   I do not use the word ' slum ' : avoid it if you can.   Its use does not minister to the self-respect of the parishioners, or to their respect for yourself.   And it is shameful to exploit the miseries of one's people to attract the attention of an indifferent or even an interested public to the heroic nature of your work or the chronic emptiness of your par-ochial coffers.   You will choose between a small parish and a large one, or a very large one, or even an enormous one.   You will choose also between a parish where there is much going on and one where there is little ; between a parish where things are fairly well in hand and one where there is very much land to be possessed; and between a parish where there is a plethora of clergymen and one which is terribly undermanned.   You will also have to consider whether the parish demands a specialist in any one branch of parochial work, or whether it requires a man of fair general capabilities.

Between these various extremes you must choose, or steer a middle course, careful while avoiding Scylla not to fall foul of Charybdis. Choose a parish of moderate and manageable size, where two or more Assistant Curates are employed ; if any lay workers are on the staff, so much the better. Go where the organization is good, but where red tape does not strangle usefulness or choke spiritual life. Go to a parish where several classes are represented, and where the work is varied in character. Go where you will get your share of preaching, not too little or too much, and where you will have plenty of visiting with the opportunity of ministering to souls. Go where there are day-schools, or at least where the work amongst the children is good.

Choose also the right Vicar. In the old days Vicars used to choose their Curates ; but all that is changed, and Curates choose their Vicars now. Whether they like it or no, Vicars must submit to the process. And as there are several curacies open to any candidate for Holy Orders who is worth his salt, it is only right that you should consider the manner of man under whom you are to work. Do not look for a man who will give you an easy time, or for one who will hold loosely the reins of spiritual or parochial direction. Look for one who is a fair preacher, visitor and organizer ; a man also of spiritual life and power; and one qualified to help and to train his colleagues. Look for a man possessed of sympathy, leadership, trust and unselfishness ; and for one who will not be moved to jealousy at the great success which you are about to win in your pastoral work, and who will not kill or even damp the enthusiasm which your fresh zeal leads you to evince for the regeneration of the parish.

You must look to your Vicar for help and guidance. Do not be vexed if he offers it at times when you do not feel the need of it. But you must be prepared to render to him loyal co-operation, to stand by him, and to support him in every possible way. Not that you are to make all his opinions your own and to sink your own individuality—there will be full scope for that to assert itself, but his position, age and experience deserve a respect which you will not be slow to exhibit. No man is perfect, and you must not expect your Vicar to be an exception to the rule. If you do not love him, you will see his defects at every turn. Even if you idolize him, you will detect them plainly enough. Do not mention them to

K

others ; and if parishioners mention them to you, refuse to be drawn. This caution gives one proof of the necessity of choosing the right parish for your first Curacy. If the choice be sound there will be less need for you to observe the caution.

At the same time, while you expect much of the Vicar, and his defects strike you as very noticeable, remember that you are raw and inexperienced, and that your Vicar will have much to put up with in you. A single mistake on your part may seriously affect his influence or retard the progress of his parochial work. And you are sure to make mistakes, but do not fear that, so long as they are not wilful or negligent. A Vicar of much experience said to me lately, " I prefer a Curate of the right sort without experience to a man of experience so-called—and this in spite of the mistakes which the man of enthusiasm will make." And though we learn by making mistakes, we ought to try to avoid them. If a man is making something and spoils it, he can throw aside the materials, and begin again with others. But it is a costly thing to spoil a soul in gaining experience.

Remember that your Vicar has to provide your stipend, and that he probably makes some

sacrifice to pay you. Be considerate then even
to a fault. Remember also that your stipend
is largely provided by the self-denial of others.
It is more pleasant to think that it comes of
the love of others for Christ than out of some
manufacture or money-making concern or
office-work ; that in many cases the devotion
of Christ's people supports us to minister to
the poor in His Name. It is a serious thing
if you turn to no spiritual account the hour
or even the minutes for which you are paid
out of the self-denial of some working-man,
or the gladly given shillings of some overworked servant. A woman in my own parish
whose income reaches only five shillings
weekly, gave last year to the Bishop of St.
Albans Fund a donation of 8s. 9d., which she
had saved in farthings, besides giving to other
objects. What a responsibility would be
incurred by the Curate, whose stipend that sum
helped to make up, if he wasted the day for
which that amount paid him. And what blessing may we not expect to follow work made
possible by the gifts of poor widows, who of
their penury give more in God's sight than the
rich? Such self-denial may enable one in a
short time to fulfil a long time.

You have now chosen your parish and the

Bishop has accepted you as a candidate for Holy Orders. You pay a visit to the parish to secure lodgings, if there be no clergy house, and to make general arrangements for taking up the work.

There are many advantages in the common life of a clergy house. Acquaintance deepens into friendship, friendship into brotherhood, brotherhood into fellowship in Christ. Here there is comfort for times of depression in the cheery spirit of a brother Curate, and at all times there is good company, good humour and good wit to be found. The instinctive sense of the eyes of others being upon us helps in the observance of the hours of parochial visitation, and in regularity and punctuality in pastoral work. This life, however, like others, has its dangers. Frivolity and foolish jesting, which are not convenient, may become too habitual; we may be tempted to keep hours of undue lateness in retiring to rest; and we may be too little with our books and most important of all—too little with God.

If you are to live in lodgings—for few of you are likely to live at first in the Vicarage or in a house of your own—ask the Vicar's advice as to the lodgings which you contemplate taking, but act entirely on your own respons-

ility.   In taking them the situation may be
bad for access to the church and to your
district; the sanitary condition of the house
may be defective; it may be sunless or dirty;
or the tenant of the house may be not quite
suitable.   If possible live in your district, but
in a healthy part of it.   A speaker at the
Liverpool Church Congress (Rev. F. W.
Head) advocated living in the midst of the
poor—if possible, in model dwellings.   A friend
of my own has settled down with his wife in
a flat in some model dwellings—Mendip
Houses, at Bethnal Green.   The name suggests bracing air and breezy heights, and I
believe that they are well and happy in their
home.   But this course is not easy, either for
an unmarried man—for where can he find
lodgings in such tenements? or for a married
man—for residence there may be difficult for
a wife and impossible for children.   Yet the
incarnation must be the guiding thought.   Our
Lord came amongst the people, shared their
lot, bore their trials and hardships; and we
must seek in our humble way to do the same.
His work was based on sacrifice—the Sacrifice
of Himself.   Our work must also be based on
sacrifice; for acceptance, for the pardon of its
imperfection, for efficacy, on the Sacrifice of

Christ ; for effect, on the sacrifice of our
selves.

Your life in your lodgings deserves attention
Your success, or rather your blessing, in the
parish will depend largely on your influence
your influence on your character ; and you
character on your self-discipline—that is, on
what you are in your personal, private and
inner life.

Character will not only make you a man of
resource, ready for emergency, but it will secure
you a hearing in many an unexpected quarter
and it will save you from many a mistake
The wellbeing of the Church depends largely
on the character of its clergy. And in that
clergy you will form a little section, with much
power to mar, if little to make their good
name. In this connection may I quote a
paragraph from the *Times* of November 16th
1891, which refers to a heathen priesthood, but
has its lessons for our own ? It is headed
" Warning a Priesthood," and runs as follows :

A proclamation recently issued by the
Japanese Minister of Home Affairs to Bud
dhist priests has excited much interest in
Japan. It is novel to find a priesthood warned
by an official, for in Japan the warnings have
usually been the other way, and it is now

centuries since a Government interfered to correct the conduct of priests. The proclamation is as follows :—" We have taken notice of the precepts of the various sects of Buddhism, and we know that they inculcate upon all priests the fostering of a sincere benevolence and a spirit of good will and forgiveness to all men ; the cure of all the souls that they can reach ; the imitation of the virtues of their departed ancestors ; the due observance of their station in life ; and the diligent preaching and propagation of the true doctrines. But we have learned that these precepts are not followed ; that partisan groups have been formed, and that there have been disgraceful struggles for worldly honours and profits. Such conduct is, surely, not worthy of priests. The directors of the sects must hereafter zealously reform their own conduct, and by their example correct the evil manners of others. Virtuous and worthy men are to be selected for the subordinate posts. The vices of extravagance and vanity are to be shunned. If these injunctions are not heeded we shall take more stringent measures. Yet such things in themselves alone will cause the dissolution of the body. The name may linger, but the strength of life will have departed. Then will its members feel only shame when they present themselves in the presence of their virtuous ancestors. We trust that there will be an immediate awakening from lethargy, and that the peace of this religious body will be strictly maintained for the future."

The warning may come home to us, " Set thine house in order : for thou shalt die, and not live " (Isaiah xxxviii. 1). " Take heed " then " unto thyself " (1 St. Timothy iv. 16), and " Take heed to the ministry which thou hast received in the Lord, that thou fulfil it " (Colossians iv. 17).

In the light of these remarks your life in your lodgings becomes of great importance. I have already spoken of rising and retiring early; begin and end the day well. Each day is a little life, and any day may be your last. Be punctual and regular at meals. So far as possible have a fixed hour for your meals, and keep to it—for the sake of your digestion as well as of your character, and for your landlady's sake. Do not bring in guests to meals, especially if extra cooking is necessary, without giving ample previous notice to your landlady. Do not give unnecessary trouble to the maid—for probably there will be only one, and she will have almost more work than she can manage. Be considerate in all things. This will secure the respect of your household, and your reputation in the parish will be enhanced. Your influence depends on your reputation as well as on your character. As regards your relation with the household amongst whom you lodge, put first the aim of winning the members, young and old, to God. Be friendly with them, but dignified. Do not be free or familiar with any young women in the house or with the maid; gain the confidence of the young men, whether sons of the house or lodgers; win the love of the children, and the respect of the landlady and her husband. Your life will mean more to them than your testimony, but the latter must come, and they cannot be won to God without it. So do not put off speaking to them of higher things. Begin on a high level, and begin so soon as possible. And when you have given your message, if it is rejected, you have delivered your soul.

Attend to details in your life in lodgings. Be careful whom you see in your own rooms. In some parishes certain young women may be glad of an excuse to see you on some private matter; it is better not to have one in your

room alone.   If the matter is too sacred to
be discussed in the presence of a third person,
refer your visitor to the Vicar ; you will then
probably find that in some mysterious way
the difficulty immediately solves itself.

Pay the charges for board and lodging regularly and punctually.   Pay ready money when
purchasing, where possible.   Be prompt in the
settlement of all other accounts ; never let one
quarter's accounts remain unpaid till the next
quarter's accounts come in.   Devote a definite
proportion of your income to God's service ;
give away neither too little, nor too much.
Keep an account of every penny which you
spend, both of your own money and of that
drawn from parochial funds.   You may find
graduated expenditure books useful.   Of parochial expenditure be careful to keep vouchers
in readiness for future audit.

The first quarter's expenses may be an
anxiety to some.   You may have just managed
to go through College and to survive a possible interval between College course and
ordination.   Then you will have to face the
question how to live during the first three
months.   The quarter will be of special expense owing to the ordination charges, the
cost of your outfit, and the moving into and

settlement in your lodgings. And, with nothing coming in for three months, bridging over the next thirteen weeks may spell endless debt. And as nothing is so damaging to bodily, mental and spiritual health as debt, your prospect of usefulness will seem altogether blighted. If the difficulty appears to be insurmountable, consult your Vicar. It will be best to do this when your first negotiations are being settled. We will suppose your stipend to be £140, with an advance to £150 on ordination as Priest. You may require an advance of £35 in monthly instalments of £15, £10 and £10. Ask your Vicar whether he will help you in this way, and promise to repay him on receipt of your stipend the sum of £6 each quarter for the first year, and £11 for the fifth quarter, if then in Priest's Orders. You have no right to *expect* your Vicar to do this. He may be unwilling to do so; he may be unable. But if he does so, his consideration merits your devotion, and he ought to receive interest in the form of increased affection from yourself.

Watch over your time as well as your money. Aim at proportion in the time which you assign to your various duties. And not only apportion your hours in prospect, but adhere to your plan in practice, and record the result in performance. Note at the end of each day how many hours you have spent in working (not dawdling or idling) over your preparation for sermons, your reading and your visiting. Your stipend does not perhaps command, but your vocation demands, your whole time.

You will probably have your mornings fairly free for preparation and for study, though not for mere amusement or for hobbies. Your afternoons and evenings will be spent in the parish. And you will not complain of your evenings being occupied, if your heart is in your work. A friend of mine had no free evening in his first Curacy of four years' duration, except when away for his annual holiday. This is a record hard to beat, and an example to avoid. The Vicar of your choice will not allow you to go on for ever. You will probably have one free day weekly, and an annual holiday of one month. This will make up a total of 78 days in the year, less than falls to a City clerk or a working man, who has his Saturday afternoons and his Sundays at home, and perhaps a week's holiday in the summer as well. But see that the average is not exceeded, and on the ground that you had no day off in the previous week do not take three days in the week following.

When you are in your own rooms, do not sit in your easy chair before your day's work is done, unless you yourself are done. We are told that St. Peter stood and warmed himself just at the moment of his temptation. Be careful not to sit over the fire and warm yourself—for more reasons than one. Read newspapers in moderation, but do not write to them, at least not without your Vicar's approval. Do not read the newspaper after breakfast, and do not spend too much time over it after lunch. Let the newspapers selected be few, but good, and general in scope, not forgetting the local. Keep in touch with public affairs in your own neighbourhood. Read the police-court news of your own district. Make the acquaintance of the defendants from your own parish, not always letting them know how much you know. It will do them good to tell their own story to you, and if they tell you nothing their conscience and your knowledge will give you the advantage in dealing with them. Do not, however, make a Bible or a god of your newspaper. Notice how little interest a newspaper of the previous day possesses, while the Bible is ever fresh and new. Yet some clergymen will spend hours over their papers, but minutes over their Bibles. If you read Church papers at all, it is better to read two than one. If your sympathies are wide, you will get a more complete view of a question. While if your antipathies are strong, 'fas et ab hoste doceri.' You will see the shortcomings of yourself and your friends, and you will get hints as to methods of work which otherwise might not reach you.

Have always some serious reading on hand, and while you do not neglect any literature which may inform the mind or help you to understand men, see that you 'draw all your studies this way.' Choose and read the right books. By all means buy what you can afford. As years pass you will probably buy less, not from want of inclination, but from want of cash. Do not be too narrow or restricted in your choice; do not confine yourself to theology on the one hand, or to fiction on the other. Be hardy. Do not lean too much on your own comforts. Be able to dispense with the pipe. Try to scorn delights, and live laborious days! " Prayer, faith and grind "—said Butler of Wantage—"will accomplish most things." And few things worth doing can be done without them.

In regard to your dress be neat and tidy at all times. Having seen men of light and leading amongst the clergy going about their work obviously unshaven, forgive a warning against allowing in yourself what would not be approved in a layman of corresponding position in social life. Make a habit of shaving when you dress, or if that be at too early an hour in winter, at any rate before breakfast. Have a cold bath on rising all the year round, if your health will stand it. And do not despise warm underclothing and a warm overcoat as well quite early in the winter. It is easier to prevent a cold than to cure one. And colds are not only apt to keep one from work for a few days at a time, but they lay the system open to worse maladies and sow the seeds of future weakness in the constitution. Do not copy the latest fashion in clerical or in unclerical attire, and on the other hand do not ape the Roman priest in the style of your hat or cut of your coat.

Forgive a few words about correspondence. The age of real letter-writing is perhaps gone for ever. With the facilities for constant communication by message or in person, and the

pressure of modern life, the art of letter-writing
has declined.   But the business of letter-writing
survives.   Take pains over your letters.   Notice
the letters of men of high standing ; observe
how concise they are.   Not a word is wasted.
The right words are chosen.   The phrases are
pregnant.   The style is simple and direct.   The
meaning is unmistakeable.   And courtesy is
shewn to the humblest correspondent.   Even
the begging letter is generally answered.   Take
trouble then over your letters.   Except when
unavoidable, never keep a letter a day without
answering it.   Tear up all letters which it is
not necessary to keep : you will thus save yourself or your survivors endless trouble.   But do
not destroy any letters of importance.   Letters
which promise you engagements keep till the
engagement has been fulfilled.   Engagements
which you make with others note in a small
pocket-book, such as one or two Life Assurance
Societies are kind enough to send out before
each new year.   And the same may well apply
to engagements which you ask others to make.
Do not leave your letters lying about, but such
as you must keep put for the time in order
of date in a large envelope.   Queen Anne's
Bounty Office keeps me supplied with just the
kind required.   When the envelope is full you

can weed out what you do not want, and classify and file the rest. A copying press and letter-book are indispensable to a Vicar, and useful to a Curate. But whereas a city office may use one or more every quarter, you will probably find a book of one thousand leaves will last you ten years. Some of you have had some experience in banks or offices, and will require no hints on the subject of order and method in correspondence. So I will add only one word : Amidst the pressure of parochial life and letters do not forget ' the old folks at home,' if God has spared to you either or both your parents. My Vicar used to find time amidst the pressure of a large South London parish, where he worked untiringly, to write to his Father once a week. And his Father as regularly wrote to him. ' Honour thy Father and thy Mother' applies to clergymen who read that Commandment as well as to young people who hear it. The time may soon come when you will be unable to hold converse with your parents, and you will then realize the value of a Father and the precious-ness of a Mother. If they can enter into the joys and sorrows of your clerical life, by all means let them share them with you. If they cannot, or if they regret the line which you

L

have taken in spiritual or ecclesiastical things; use regularly this opportunity of shewing your undiminished affection for them. Even if the utmost divergences exist, never forget that you owe to them under God your actual existence; the possibility of sharing in that Sonship of God, which the Father has extended to men in Christ; beside the influence of example and early training, and the much prized opportunity, in part or in whole, of entering the Ministry of the Church. Remember your physical, mental, social, spiritual and financial debt to them. And though you have as a clergyman a responsibility for your teaching and practice and conduct of which you cannot divest yourself, try in all things reasonable to meet their wishes, and refrain from what might grieve them, if it be not necessary to engage in it. At any rate write to them ; write fully, freely, lovingly, and confidentially. And do not let it have to be said of you, as I once heard said of an officer in the Army by his Father, " When I see a letter from my son, I know that he wants money."

The explanation of the Ten Commandments given in the Church Catechism under the head of our Duty towards our Neighbour includes in the scope of the Fifth Commandment not only our parents, but also our rulers and betters, our spiritual pastors and masters. The younger clergy do not always seem to me to shew sufficient deference to age and experience. They expect a respectful hearing when their turn comes—or does not come—to offer their expressions of opinion. If their views are so mature, perhaps even infallible, at so early an age as thirty years, who can estimate the attention which their utterances will deserve when they reach the age of seventy, seventy-five, or even eighty years? Yet an aged servant of Christ, who perhaps at thirty years of age was twice as learned and thrice as spiritually minded as these junior clergymen, on rising to speak in a Synod or Ruri-Decanal Conference out of the fulness of a long and rich experience, with the added grace which comes from conscious nearness to the world to come, is listened to with scant courtesy and scarcely veiled impatience by the younger clergy. Respect in personal intercourse and in correspondence ought surely to be accompanied by respect in synod or assembly.

Regarding your relations with the Bishop I need say little. It is possible that he may have so very large a number of men working under him that he may scarcely be able to do more than know you. But you need not on that account feel debarred from access to him, and in your first Curacy at least you will be more than a name to him. Do not trouble him over unnecessary matters, and do not push yourself under his notice every time you happen to be present at some epis-copal function. But it will be a great comfort to you if you can feel that he is at your back supporting you in your work with the weight of his influence and approval. He is the chief Pastor of the diocese, and if you are faithful as a Pastor under him your work will cheer and encourage him. If you contemplate removing to another Curacy, going to the Mission-field, or even accepting a living, lay the matter before him as your spiritual chief.

I have already spoken of your relations with your Vicar and with your fellow Assis-tant-Curates. In your ordinary work do not hesitate to consult your Vicar at every turn, tell him of your own spiritual difficulties, let him share with you the joy of seeing a sinner brought to repentance under your influence; but do not trouble him at incon-venient times, do not feel rebuffed if he

ever has to bring your interview to a conclusion, do not dawdle in his study after you
have said your say. If you have any griev-
ance, talk the matter over with him. If he
does not sanction all your projects, do not
suspect him of want of appreciation of your
zeal.

Remember that he has to consider the
parish as a whole, while your eyes are upon
the field that you reap and the sheep which
you tend. If you have a Mission-Church
under your charge be loyal to your Vicar
there, remember that he is the Vicar there
as well as in the Parish Church. Do not
deviate from the Parish Church usage in
ways that might evoke from Parish Church
folk discontent with their lot, nor allow your
work or methods to reflect on the standard
of the Parish Church. Do not isolate your
Mission Church, keep it in touch with the
rest of the parish. In fact keep the unity of
the parish in the bond of peace. Keep your
Vicar informed, says Canon Savage (*Pastoral
Visitation*, ch. ii. p. 30), " concerning the
condition of things in the parish." Some
Vicars may not appreciate your kindness.
Even if you tell *them* less, do not keep
back information of vital importance.

You may at times long for a word of sympathy, encouragement, or praise from your Vicar, and may long in vain. Do not be discouraged at this. He may be a man of few words, or not given to much praise. This is a pity, but it is better that he should be such than given to flattery or to the fostering of self-conceit. And words of encouragement when they do come from such a man are of more value than gushing commendation and fulsome praise. An undeserved rebuke from the Vicar may chill or wound a loyal and brave soul, though one is not always the best judge as to the needlessness of the rebuke. There must, however, be a spirit of unity between you and your Vicar. How can you expect unity to prevail amongst the people, if they note its absence from their leaders? The same holds good of your relations with your fellow Assistant-Curates. There must be the spirit of unity between you and amongst you all, if blessing is to be commanded from above. Do not be continually criticizing one another. Help each other by all means, point out failings, but speak the truth in love, in honour preferring one another and each esteeming other better than himself. Let there be devotional intercourse, and that in addition to the union in worship in church. Pray with one another, and speak to one another of the things of God and of your own spiritual experience.

> "Behold, how good and how pleasant it is
> For brethren to dwell together in unity!
> It is like the precious oil upon the head,
> That ran down upon the beard,
> Even Aaron's beard;
> That came down upon the skirt of his garments;
> Like the dew of Hermon,
> That cometh down upon the mountains of Zion:
> For there the Lord commanded the blessing,
> Even life for evermore" (Psalm cxxxiii., R.V.).

In a large parish there may be lay-workers on the parochial staff, male or female, paid or honorary. Be careful to maintain brotherly relations with them. Let the Lay-reader, the Scripture-reader or the City Missionary feel that he is one with you. He may feel the need of sympathy even more than you do. His work is probably more difficult than yours, while his position is more isolated and more precarious. As regards Nurses or Mission-women, be dignified in your relations with them. Never descend to frivolity or familiarity. Be careful how and how often you visit each other. Do not go to tea alone with the mission-woman or read Shakespeare together. Do not give occasion to the enemy to blaspheme. What is perfectly lawful may not be expedient. 'Avoid every appearance of evil' is good advice even if not a literal translation of words of St. Paul.

Churchwardens and Sidesmen will find you courteous, sympathetic and appreciative. Look up to them and esteem them very highly for their work's sake. Associate them with the spiritualities, as well as the temporalities of the parish. Draw them closer to the Vicar. Let them discern in you a spiritual tone, and help them to develope a sense of the solemnity of their office.

You will be brought into touch with the Organist and Choir. You may be able to devote time to them which the Vicar can ill spare. You may join them at Choir practice or visit them in their own homes. Keep them loyal to the Vicar, and content with the liberty and scope which he assigns them. Set before them high ideals. Teach them the nature of worship and the meaning of praise. Remind them that they that bear the vessels of the Lord must be clean. "Whoso offereth praise glorifieth me: and to him that ordereth his conversation aright will I shew the salvation of God" (Psalm l. 23). "So we Thy people, and sheep of Thy pasture, will give Thee thanks for ever ; we will shew forth Thy praise to all generations " (Psalm lxxix. 13).

You will also work in harmony with a large body of voluntary workers of all kinds. They will deserve your respect. Their work is a labour of love. And in large and poor parishes you will often find that the best workers are those who are already overpressed with their daily toil. As ill paid and poor folk will sometimes give of their penury to the treasury of God, so overworked and tired men and women will sacrifice the remnants of their time —so often needed for fresh air or rest—to the glory of God. It is such offerings which are specially acceptable to God, and ascend to Him as a sweet savour of Christ. You are paid to give your whole working time to the work ; your freshness of body and mind are devoted to it; you are called of God to be the shepherd of these souls. Try then to inspire and stimu-late them. Appreciate, thank and encourage them. Teach them that their work is done for the Lord, and not for the clergy or even for the Church. While not withholding yourself from young men, do not make yourself too cheap to them. Encourage self-respect in young women, as well as respect for the clergy. Be careful how you conduct yourself with children and especially with young girls. Keep ever in view your office to train and perfect the saints for their work of ministry with a view to building up the Body of Christ.

The officials of the church will be more or less at your beck and call. Do not be domineering over them : do not order them about. Be civil and kindly. If you see a fault, speak gently to them. Report it to the Vicar, only if too serious to be passed over. Do not put them out of their position, lest by your own excess of friendliness they be tempted to forget themselves when receiving instructions from the Vicar.

As for yourself be punctual in your parish engagements. Allow yourself time. Start rather sooner than you need, and then an interruption will not cause you to be late. Do not be always on the rush. Do not arrive at the last minute, or the last minute but one, or the minute after the last. Even if in a hurry, do not appear so. Give callers time to explain the object of their calls, and if weakness or old age makes them prolix or slow, have patience with them, and they will tell you all. Let people tell their own story and do not mind occasionally hearing what you know already. The mere unburdening of their troubles may

do them good.   Samuel Wilberforce wrote his
resolution on becoming Bishop of Oxford
(*Biography*, volume i. p. 320): "Never to
hurry men who come to consult you.   Mere
venting themselves is a relief.   The receiving
of this is a duty of sympathy."   Do not keep
old people, or indeed any people, standing.
Do not keep them waiting longer than you
can help, or you may forget that they are
there.   Even a poor woman who has come
begging because her children are ill and her
husband is out of work, may have important duties awaiting her at home, or her
children may be too young or too ill to
be left for more than a few minutes at a
time.

In all your pastoral relations—in the lodgings or the parish, the Vicarage or the homes
of the people, the church or the parish room,
the schools or the open air, remember Jesus
Christ.   Cultivate both the bearing of the
Christian and the bearing of the Cross.   You
may have either or neither, but you ought to
have both.   You may be exact and business-
like, regular and punctual—even punctilious
in keeping your engagements, and meet
with few rebuffs.   But there ought to be a
Cross to bear.   If you have none, you are

probably making little impression on the world, or its hostility would be aroused. Be to your people what Christ would have you be. Do not study merely the impressions which you leave on people's minds. Be yourself. To your own self be true. Above all be true to Christ. Your life will then speak. Your character will make its own impression. And each parishioner will be moved to say, even if he rejects your ministry, "Behold now, I perceive that this is an holy man of God which passeth by us continually" (2 Kings iv. 9).

There is one sphere outside your pastoral relationship which must not be passed by. We complain that some people are apt to leave their religion behind when they leave church, or when Sunday is over. Be careful not to leave your religion behind when you leave your parish. You may be going to see friends or to do some shopping; you may have private business to transact, to visit the dentist or a medical man; you may be going up to or into London, to the country or to the seaside; you may be having a day off at cricket or golf; you may be away for a few days or for your annual holiday. But, wherever you are, remember that you are a servant of Christ, and have a mission from Christ. Your garb proclaims you to be a clergyman. If you lay aside clerical dress for a time, discard it not merely to enjoy a certain laxity, which you could not otherwise allow yourself. But where you are recognized as a clergyman, if for no higher motive than the interests of the clergyman in charge of the place where you are or of the people with whom for the moment you come into contact, remember the sanctity and the honour of your calling. Try to take a higher view than that. At all times it is your duty to be about your Father's business. And even if you are amongst them as no more than a layman, remember the general commission of the layman as well as the special commission of the clergyman. You will be a man amongst men as well as a parson, a Christian as well as a priest, a layman as well as a clergyman. In these relationships let your conversation be seasoned with salt, and such as becometh the Gospel of Christ. Consistency when off duties is sure of its reward.

In all things—inside the parish and outside it—seek to approve yourselves as ministers of Christ, giving offence in nothing, that the ministry be not blamed. Take trouble over the smallest details, and over the humblest parishioners. Do not waste time over them, but give time to them. "Whatsoever thy hand findeth to do, do it with thy might" (Ecclesiastes ix. 10). A good thing done badly may appear less attractive than a bad thing done well. Put your very best into everything you do. Some months ago a young railwayman was knocked down and killed by a light engine just outside St. Pancras Station. The body of the poor fellow was brought to our churchyard for burial, followed by a number of his mates. One of my colleagues conducted the service. Soon after the service was finished I happened to pass the door of a public-house opposite the church, where some of the mourners were seated. As I passed the door I heard one say, " Didn't he read the service impressive?" That remark coming from such a quarter was not without its value. Genius, we are told, is an infinite capacity for taking pains. "Serve truly and painfully"—as runs the Bidding Prayer in Canon 55. In all depart- ments of life the demand is for efficiency, and the efficient win the day. In the workshop of the minister of Christ the same law holds good. "Study to shew thyself approved unto God, a workman that needeth not to be ashamed" (2 St. Timothy ii. 15). Do not shrink from wearing work. Take it up boldly. Thank God for it. And in your pastoral relationship with all sorts and conditions of men, act as the true pastor at all times, however weary, however poorly, however pressed. Be to your people like Jesus Christ, and not least like Him in this, "the same yesterday, and to-day, and for ever."

VI.

THE PASTOR AS A PREACHER.

FROM several quarters light has recently beat about the Church of England pulpit in London. And though the light has been somewhat fierce, is has not been altogether unfriendly. We shall be better employed in weighing the conclusions of the luminaries than in explaining them away. Mr. Mudie-Smith, who organized, in connection with the *Daily News*, the recent Church attendance census throughout London, tells us that the Church of England is losing ground in London. It is useless to meet this assertion with a bare negative, for he adduces facts and figures in support of his conclusions. Not only does the Church of England fail, he says, to keep pace with the growth of the population so far as the number of actual adherents goes, but it scarcely stands where it did nineteen years ago. He attributes this mainly to failure in preaching

ower. The churches in which preaching is a
eading factor shew a better record of attend-
nce than other churches. Moreover, men
ttend in large numbers where the pulpit is a
ower. This is borne out by comparative
tatistics. It will be readily admitted that the
Nonconformists make more of preaching than
oes the Church. How then do they stand?
Ve learn that some 153,000 men were
numerated as present at worship in London
hurches as against some 216,000 at Noncon-
ormist places of worship. At the same time
he women present at churches outnumbered the
vomen at chapels by 292,000 as against 93,000.
That means that for every two women who
ço to a church in London there is one man,
ut for every two women who go to a chapel
here are nearly five men. The same propor-
ion of men to women in the Church of Eng-
and as we find in the Nonconformist denomi-
ations would give a total of 677,000 men
nstead of 153,000. This can only mean that
ur men stay away from church in great
umbers.

Other luminaries throw further light on the
ituation. The *Daily Telegraph* summed up in
n impartial article the conclusions drawn from
ts correspondence of 10,000 letters on the

M

question, " Do we believe ? " It asserted tha
at heart the English people were still sound
but that the clergy had been content to repea
formulae satisfactory to themselves, though no
so to those who are still anxious to call them
selves Christians. There was a curious inequality
between "what earnest and reverent mei
demand at the present day and what equally
earnest and reverent but somewhat narrow
minded clergymen are able to supply " (*Daily
Telegraph*, 31st December, 1904). Advertins
from the general to the particular this con
tention is borne out by a volume which was
recently published with the title, *The Diary o,
a Churchgoer*. To some extent the writer puts
himself out of court by avowing himself as no
being a communicant, and further as being at
least hazy on the subject of our Lord's Divinity
But he is open to conviction. He longs to get
from the pulpit that which he rarely receives—
light from another world. When the clergyman
is at the lectern, various contributing causes
lead him to say within himself, " This thing is
of God." But he cannot always say the same
when the clergyman speaks from the pulpit.
More important than the symptom of this
writer's complaint is the view taken by the
Times reviewer of the book, who says that

the English clergy speak more often than they
realize to men who are open to conviction and
are supremely worth convincing. Many are
waiting for light from another world. If we
can shew it to them and if they can see in us
Christ the Light of the world, they will listen
to what we have to tell, in a word—to our
preaching. We may be able to prove to our
own satisfaction that we are teachers sent from
God. But few people who are not already
convinced will accept us on that account. Our
credentials may receive less attention than they
deserve. And even if people are assured of
our authority, it does not follow that they will
act upon our preaching. But if God be in us
they will be compelled to listen, and they will
not ask for proof of our authority to speak.
After all the chief function of an ἀπόστολος is to
deliver the message of him who sends him.
Else wherefore sent ?   An ἀπόστολος must have
something to tell.

In pioneer or missionary work it is obvious
that the work of preaching takes precedence.
The evangelist is all important. But when the
Gospel has been received, and the Church has
been planted, and a settled ministry obtains,
the delivery of God's message and the interpre-
tation of His will and the application of His

truth to the needs of men are still of first importance.

The popularity of preaching or of a particular preacher does not affect the question. Nor is it affected by our like or dislike of the work. Our first duty is to be Ministers of the Word. This is not of chance, but of choice. It was not always so in our own Church. And a general decrease in preaching power may be due to a lowered estimate of its importance.

Persuading men to be reconciled to God and bringing Christianity into relation with life will task to the utmost the powers of a clergyman. He may be thankful if he has power in either connection. And when we add the teaching of doctrine, the arousing, quickening, stimulating and deepening of various classes of hearers, we are naming more difficulties which the preacher has to face.

In parishes where the Church is strong, the pulpit is a power. From it radiates an influence which is felt in every branch of the work and in every quarter of the parish. This influence may be so strong in some cases that defective pastoral work and organization may seem to be atoned for and to be compensated for by the power exerted through the Vicar's preaching. We notice also that in many parishes excellent organization and diligent visiting do not build up the Church, when the preaching is admittedly weak. The ideal is for the pulpit to be a power, and for its influence to be supported and followed up by method in parochial work and by special care for individual souls.

The distinction between preparation for preaching and the preparation of a sermon will be obvious. Both are important. For what is the criterion of success in a preacher? Not eloquence assuredly, but effectiveness in bringing men and women face to face with God and in making them lead different lives. For this end preparation of a sermon is not enough. Neither is preparation for preaching enough by itself.

Wherein does preparation for preaching lie?

There is a certain common factor to the preparation for all pastoral work and therefore for preaching, of which I have already spoken. The preacher must be a man of God and must understand men. Allowing for that, preparation for preaching takes place in a man's own heart; in his parish; in his schools; and in his study.

The preacher must speak out of his own personal experience and knowledge. Else the element of life and the ring of sincerity will be wanting from his preaching. His sermons will become mere exposition of the theory of religion. They will do actual harm to the hearers—such as there will be—by not applying religion to their daily life. They will make religion a dry subject. Religion need never be dry. What other subject could hold the attention of hundreds of thousands of hearers twice a Sunday, week by week, year after year? You may wonder how you can go on preaching for years and years and still have something fresh to say. The fault will be your own if your fears find fulfilment. When Christ is preached, religion always has its attraction. If you are often speaking on one particular subject, such as Temperance, or the work of some religious society, it may be hard to find continually something fresh to say. But if your heart is in communion with God and filled with love for men, you will never want a message to give in the Master's name. I spoke of knowledge and experience as being a factor in preparation for preaching. Never preach what you do not sincerely believe to be true. To some extent you will be dependent on others, experts in various branches of history, science or theology. But you will have taken pains to arrive at your own position before you attempt to teach others.

Do not preach beyond your own experience. You cannot speak of the peace of God if you do not know it in your own heart. The joy of the Lord must have filled your soul before you can describe it to others. You cannot tell of the forgiveness of sins unless you know that your own are forgiven. You cannot tell of the victory over sin which Christ gives unless you are experiencing His power against the temptations of daily life. If your own spiritual experience be meagre, your hearers will suffer. The remedy is to raise the standard of your spiritual experience. And by the grace of God this can be done. But at all costs be true to yourself. The danger of unreality may be difficult to avoid in united expressions of prayer or praise. One standard has then to be fitted to numerous varieties of experience. Our people may sing

> "Oh we long to know
> The triumph-song of heaven,"

when many of them have no such wish. But the preacher may not say so unless he really feels it. And if he does really feel this wish, many of his hearers will begin to feel it too.

Do not preach beyond your experience, but

on the other hand do not preach below your experience. If you believe a thing and if it will help the people to know that you believe it, do not be afraid to tell them. If Christ has come to mean more and to be more to you, say so in the pulpit. A preacher must be willing to wear his heart on his sleeve. The batteries from which he fires must be unmasked. The hearers must be able to see the guns. For they are friends not foes, and the fire is meant to deal not death but life amongst those whom it lays low. To reveal, to lay bare yourself may cost you much. It may lay you open to the charge of inconsistency. But it must be done. The effect upon yourself may be humbling—all the better. But at all costs you must give yourself to your people, as much in the pulpit as in the parish. " The gift without the giver is bare." Does not failure here impress you in many a church? You hear a sermon—all is excellent. You feel that the preacher is a good sincere man. But there is not that indescribable sympathy between him and yourself which is felt in listening to some preachers. The preacher is keeping himself back from the congregation. It may be shyness which retards him or that reserve which is so marked a feature of British character. But he is

study worthy of the name takes place, and in
some parishes, to gain a quiet time for study,
the study is the one room which it is necessary
to forsake.   The exigences of modern parochial
life turn the study into a sort of office.   Here
numbers of parochial accounts are kept; perhaps
a hundred letters a week are written; thousands
of notices and circulars are sent out at different
times; several score of parishioners are inter-
viewed in the course of a month; and all kinds
of parochial lumber are stored.   All this has an
effect on preaching.   I have already spoken of
the disadvantage at which the Church of
England clergy appear as contrasted with their
Nonconformist brethren.   Mr. Charles Booth
suggests a possible reason for the contrast when
he sketches the morning of a parochial clergyman and that of a Congregational minister.
Neither is wholly right or wholly wrong.   A
morning of mere study may tend to a certain
aloofness from human suffering and sorrow,
while a morning of business or of attention
to those who have a right to ask our counsel
may preclude that attention to reading which
St. Paul commends to us.   But there is
something wrong when the working day of
an English clergyman becomes so proverbial as
to warrant the remark of the *Times*, apropos of

a volume of Canon Ainger's sermons, "Imagine
Ainger at the head of some great London
parish, cumbered about with much serving of
tables. . . . A happier fate decided that he
should be a preacher. . . . It is possible that
he would have distributed coal-tickets or
exhorted a mothers' meeting to admiration, it
is enough that he could preach to a cultured
congregation what was good for the use of
edifying" (*Times*, 4th November, 1904).

The blame for inattention to reading cannot
be laid wholly at the door of the parish. The
Guardian in a very sensible article last year
(7th September, 1904) pointed out that some
of the busiest statesmen make time to study
and that the clergy ought to do the same;
want of desire to read is quite as much to
blame as want of time; one hour a day will
make a difference in a year. So says the
Guardian, and it ought to know. A hearty
desire to read is something for which we ought
to pray. Whoever else can afford not to read,
the preacher cannot.

The study of the Bible must hold the first
place. In fact we are to draw all our studies
that way. The pulpit and the Book which
lies in it are to be our objective. Study may
not make a man a better celebrant, but

it will make him a better preacher. There is, however, one important link between the Lord's Table and the pulpit. The Holy Communion is a 'proclamation,' a 'shewing' of the Lord's Death (1 Corinthians xi. 26). Different truths may be emphasized in different ages, but the Holy Communion keeps us close to the central fact in Christian doctrine—the Death of Christ. In our preaching then the Death of Christ must be the keynote. "We preach Christ crucified." The atonement and the personal blessing which it brings—pardon through the precious Blood of Christ—must have the chief place. As at the Holy Table, so in the pulpit; and as in the pulpit, so in the study. We must try to grasp the scheme of Christian doctrine, taking the Death of Christ as the central point.

In choice of subjects for reading and study the clergyman must observe a wise economy. For guidance as to details he need be at no loss, what with outlines of study such as Bishop Ellicott gives in his excellent books on Sacred Study [1] or the hints which the Society of Sacred Study gives. The point which I wish to press is the observance of due proportion. Do not live too much in your church, your parish, or

[1] *Foundations of Sacred Study*, two volumes—S.P.C.K.

your study. And when in your study do not
spend all the time over your correspondence
or general parish business, but give a fair share
of time to study, and in study put things in
their proper places.

From time to time it will be your duty to
prepare a sermon. How often you will be
called on to preach will depend on the character
of the parish, and on possible restrictions of
your Bishop. In any case you will not be
in a position to do as Bishop Westcott did,
when Canon of Westminster—to spend a
fortnight over each sermon, and to refuse to
preach more sermons than he could fully
prepare (*Life*, vol. ii. ch. ix. p. 36). But Dr.
Westcott's practice will remind us of the
importance of carefully preparing every sermon.
Though sometimes forgotten, that is an axiom
which none will dispute. What will be your
procedure ? At the close of each month you
will receive from your Vicar a scheme of the
sermons to be preached during the following
month. You sit down to prepare the first of
these. First choose a text or a subject. You
may wish to bring some special subject before
your people. Even then you will choose a text
at least to introduce it. Be careful not to make
the text a mere motto—a figure-head to adorn

your ship. You are to give a message from God each time you preach, and it will be the rarest thing for a message from God not to be best expressed in the form of a text from His Word.

Choose your text so long beforehand as possible. Be sure that it contains the message which God would have you give. Otherwise you will produce a 'laboured' sermon, which will be heavy to both preacher and hearer. Pray for guidance on each occasion. One may come in a moment. But do not grudge time, even an hour, in choosing a text. You may have a list of texts or subjects which have come to you in the course of previous study or meditation or pastoral work. Note them in a Calendar against the date for which they will be suitable. The sight of Herbert Schmalz' 'Return from Calvary' gave me subjects for the whole of Holy Week and Easter one year. The reading of such a book as *Pastor Pastorum* will provide a whole sheaf of subjects. In any case you need never be hard up for a subject. Some years ago a book was published entitled, *The Parson's Perplexity, or, What to Preach About*. But surely so much comes within the range of the Bible that it is more difficult to know what not to preach about. Of course if a man be not sent, he cannot preach. "How shall they preach, except they be sent?" (Romans x. 15).

You have your text. Begin your sermon. Whether you preach extempore or not, it will be better to write your sermon out. But before you write it, get the idea of the sermon with its outline worked out. Be very particular about the opening and closing sentences. Let the first few sentences be connected with the main thought of the sermon, yet let them contain something of human interest which will arrest the attention of hearers. Having won their attention at the outset you will find it easier to keep it all through. The close of the sermon is also of great importance. Our sermons are apt to fail in application. But in our closing sentences we want to bring home and fasten on the hearer the truth which we have brought to light in the course of our sermon. As for the main body of the sermon, see that the arrangement is natural, giving not your own ideas, but those of the text ; see that the connection is likely to be obvious to the hearer, and the sequence of thought gentle and easy. Remember that you have better educated hearers than you would

have had years ago.   They will therefore grasp
an idea more quickly, and you will have less
need to elaborate a subject.   At the same time
the present generation has not so good listeners
as a previous one.   You will therefore on both
grounds need to occupy a shorter period in
preaching a sermon than did the clergyman of
the last century.   Set down before you make
your analysis all you can think of respecting the
text, praying that the Holy Spirit may direct
and rule your thoughts.   And when you have
exhausted your own resources, then read
carefully and note afterwards what commentators or other writers have to say upon the
passage.   When you have completed your
notes, carefully read over and classify and
arrange them, and complete your analysis.
Arrange your sermon under the old-fashioned
heads, but it may be better not to announce
the heads, or at any rate not their numerical
order.   If the body is to live the bones
must be there, though they need not be seen.
If there must be a 'lastly,' let one be enough
for one sermon.   You can then add one or
two illustrations to lighten and illuminate your
sermon.

The choice of illustrations is a subject in
itself.   Do not adopt any short cut in the use

N

of them. The employment of illustrations drawn from specially compiled books is generally as inadvisable as that of ready-made outlines of sermons. Look out for your own illustrations. If brief and pointed, they will be more telling than those drawn from a book. Do not tell as anecdotes things which never actually happened. Let the heroes of your illustrations be men rather than women or children. Let one good illustration be enough for a single point. Be careful about the technique of your illustrations. If you are giving an illustration drawn from facts within your own knowledge, be careful about the details. You may make some error of fact or detail which will fix the mind of a hearer who knows on your mistake rather than on the truth which you are applying. On one occasion I illustrated the reunion of the disciples after the Resurrection by the story of the reunion of friends and relations at Portsmouth two days after they had said farewell to the officers and men of a cruiser proceeding to Australia. Their reunion at Portsmouth in joy two days after scattering to their own homes in sorrow could only mean that their loved ones had unexpectedly returned. This was what had actually occurred. The engines of the cruiser had broken down, and she had put back for repairs. After preaching the sermon in which I described the incident I learned that some relatives of one of the officers on board were in church. I felt at least thankful that the picture was not overdrawn and that nothing had been said reflecting on the persons mentioned.

Do not quote often in sermons. The opinions of others may be more valuable than his own, but a preacher loses hold if he cites them too often.[1] When you do quote, quote poetry rather than prose, and let the quotation be brief. Canon Beeching tells a story of Canon Ainger preaching at the Temple one gloomy February afternoon. The congregation was afflicted with an epidemic of coughing and the preacher could scarcely be heard. At a certain point he introduced a line from Macbeth

> " the eyes are open
> Ay, but their sense is shut,"

spoken as only he could speak it, and as if by magic the coughing ceased, and the rest of the sermon was listened to in peace (*The Gospel and Human Life*, Preface, pp. vii, viii).

Do not overload your sermons, and resist the temptation to put into one sermon what had better be kept for another. Bishop Jacobson

[1] See *Pastor Pastorum*, p. 209.

of Chester used to warn his Ordination candi
dates not to cram all their Divinity into thei
first sermon. At the same time see that there
is something for the hungry sheep to feed or
and to take away.

When writing out your sermon, remember
that it must be plainly legible in the dim
religious light of the pulpit. Rewrite rather
than write between the lines. Let your altera
tions be unmistakable. It is sometimes wel
to enclose in a circle any erasure ; the eye wil
then more readily pass it by. Write your
sermon as if you were writing in the pulpit with
the people before you, but do not think that the
moment it is written you are ready to enter the
pulpit. Go over it carefully with thought and
prayer. Cut out what is redundant or other
wise unnecessary. See that your meaning is
absolutely clear. Some hearers will invert
your meaning in their own minds if they
possibly can. A Liberal candidate was recently
addressing a political meeting in a country town.
His remarks ran somewhat as follows :—" I
Mr. Chamberlain's scheme were carried out
you labourers would probably get 8s. or 9s. a
week, and bread would be 1s. a loaf." After
the meeting he asked an old labourer for his
vote. All he could get was, " You needn't

think I'm a'going to give you my vote, if you be going to bring back them old times." Be simple in your language at all times, especially in preaching to uneducated people.

Whatever the subject of your sermons be, preach Christ. Tell the people what He has done, is doing and will do for them. Preach Him in His Incarnation, in ' His Cross and Passion, in His precious Death and Burial, in His glorious Resurrection and Ascension.' Preach the word of reconciliation. Inculcate deep views of the guilt of sin. Do not minimise death, judgment and punishment hereafter. Preach the law and preach repentance, whereby we forsake sin. Tell the people they must be born again—not only of water but also of the Holy Ghost. Preach faith in our Blessed Lord as the means of obtaining salvation. Preach holiness without which no man shall see the Lord. Distinguish between justification and sanctification. Magnify the grace of God and honour the Holy Ghost. Preach the Christian's duty towards God, and his duty towards his neighbour. So far as in you lies, declare in course of time the whole counsel of God. Note the subjects which you treat from time to time, in order that the various doctrines of the faith may be brought before your people. Do not make a hobby horse of one pet phrase, doctrine or subject, and forthwith ride him to death. Do not let your fourth sermon be practically a repetition of your first, with just a different text. Have something fresh to say each time you preach. Do not prepare so long a sermon that you will weary your hearers, or so short that you can scarcely touch the fringe of your subject. When you have said all you have to say, finish your sermon. It is better to send people away wanting more, than feeling that they have had too much. Aim at getting people to think. Leave them sometimes to draw their own conclusions, always taking care that it shall be possible for them to draw no other than the right one. Do not preach to parents on the management of children if you are unmarried, and do not address your older hearers as if you were of their age or experience, nor on the other hand as if you thought that a hearer was ' aged ' at sixty. Be careful in references which may remind some hearers of great sorrows in their lives. A Deacon some time ago touched in a sermon on the loss of little children. It did not comfort a mother who had a few years before lost her infant son to hear the preacher say that the calling away of a little child might mean his being saved from prison life in after years. Put yourself in the position of your hearers. Ask yourself what impression your words would leave on you if you were a hearer instead of the preacher.

You will probably bring special subjects before your people in Lent. In Advent preach specially on the Second Coming of our Lord. The preaching of Advent sermons and the interest taken in them is a fair test of the spiritual character of a congregation. There is a paucity of really helpful books on the Second Advent, perhaps because the field of prophecy is so little entered by clergy to-day, but I can recommend highly an inexpensive book by Canon Flynn, published by Elliot Stock in 1898, entitled *Studies in the Second Advent*.

The time at length comes for the sermon to be preached. Is it to be delivered extempore or from manuscript? It is impossible to lay down an absolute rule, but generally speaking it is best to preach from brief notes. This may be qualified by saying that during the first year in many cases it is advisable to preach from manuscript in one's parish church. It is true that Canon Liddon preached his sermons in St. Paul's from manuscript, but he was a man by himself, and—as his biographer tells us—even he in his earlier years preached extempore. Precede your sermon with private prayer that you may be cleansed and fitted to speak, and that the Holy Spirit may give you utterance and the people grace to hear. Stand erect in the pulpit, not too stiffly nor continually bobbing about. Let your attitude be easy, and just talk to the people in a natural tone. Do not be afraid of shewing feeling, though you will be the last to simulate it. While careful not to wander from the point, do not be afraid of being carried away with your subject.

A London paper in a report of a recent meeting spoke of "a rather uninspired number of speeches . . . by clergymen, who, great as their authority and influence are, have not the power of converting zeal into fervour, or devotion into enthusiasm" (*Daily Graphic*, 6th February, 1905). That is one weak point of our preaching. We want more fire in our pulpits; we are too respectable, too little affected by the awfulness of sin, the love of Christ, and our responsibility for the people's souls. We forget that some may be hearing the Gospel for the first or the last time. On my second Sunday evening in my former incumbency I little thought while preaching that one of the congregation would pass away before reaching home after service.

We need the outpouring of the Holy Ghost, that we may preach with power to move men's hearts. God is teaching the clergy solemn lessons. He is using a young Welsh collier, an American Congregationalist minister, a self-taught Gipsy to change the lives of thousands of our fellow-countrymen, where the clergy seem able only to move their hundreds. We need to get down on our knees before ordination as Evan Roberts did when a Divinity student and seek a power which most of us readily confess we know not. And it is a sign to be thankful for that the Archbishop of Canterbury is appointing a day for solemn waiting upon God by the clergy and laity that the Holy Spirit may be poured out upon our Church. Rely upon the Holy Spirit and believe that He is able to touch your hearers' hearts. Remember that eloquence does not make a good sermon, and that your object is not to make your hearers enjoy your sermon, but really to move their hearts. With this end in view make your remarks personal, while avoiding personalities. Press the point right home. Your hearers will parry the remarks if they can. A gentleman who attended church when staying at his country house wrote to a Vicar on his leaving the parish : "Your sermons have appeared to me to be well suited to the class of people you have addressed." He did not seem to include himself in the number.

Keep your eye on your people the whole time. Canon Liddon evidently thought this most important. Hear what he says in his diary of a sermon preached at the age of 34 : "Felt that my preparation was incomplete, and that I kept my eye too much upon the paper. There was also a want of unction. I did not feel frequently what I was saying" (*Life*, p. 68). The *Times* recently published an article on the Welsh Revival. Of the central figure in the movement it said : "One thing rivetted attention. The eyes seemed to fasten on the congregation with a glare and a grip. I heard a collier describe the same impression thus : 'He looks that fixed on you, and never pulls his eyes off you'" (3rd January, 1905). There is much in the power of the eye as well as in that of the voice.

I might sum up the requirements in a preacher after the manner of Canon Twells— himself a preacher of first rank (*Colloquies on Preaching*, p. 72)—a consistent and conscientious life; a real love for souls; a constant habit of intercessory prayer; an accurate acquaintance with the Word of God; a knowledge of ancient and modern writers; close observation of men's characters; a clear voice; a persuasive manner; and a chastened judgment.

While we are tempted to ask, Who is sufficient for these things? and to feel that success is impossible, 'let us remember Jesus Christ.' The effect of a speech depends partly on the power of the speaker, partly on the character of the hearers. So with preaching, if we give due place to the Holy Spirit. If success depended only on the speaker, in our Lord's case all hearers would have been won. They heard a perfect Gospel expounded in a perfect manner by a perfect Man. Yet all did not believe. Can we be surprised if many reject our message? But we can at least aim at improvement in our understanding and our presentation of the Gospel, and in our own personal character.

And let us remember the need of courage. The preacher must be willing to stand alone, to speak out boldly, and to be—if you like— in advance of the age. Some seventy years ago there were serious riots at Bristol on the questions raised by the Reform Bill. Danger threatened the Cathedral and its precincts. A Minor Canon suggested to Bishop Gray that service had better be postponed. "My young friend," said the Bishop, "there are times in which it is necessary not to shirk danger; our duty is to be at our post." The Bishop preached. Before evening the Palace was burnt down, and the Bishop lost his papers and property to the value of £10,000 (*Southey's Life*, vi. p. 167).

Of preaching to special classes much might be said. In speaking about preaching to men I do not enter into the important subject of organizing men's services. That is quite an art in itself, and has been well described by Mr. Watts Ditchfield in his book *Fishers of Men*, and by Mr. Swainson in his book on Bible-Class work. But I assume that you have got your men—no easy task in any large number, and proceed to address them. You will probably have the subject of your sermon printed on cards or bills. Be careful not to choose titles which will cheapen religion in the eyes of parishioners, nor to print the Sacred Name on cards which may be thrown in the gutter. Speak to the men with as few notes as possible, straightly and frankly, as picturesquely as possible but not too colloquially.   In ordinary respects you will address men as you would any other congregation, and if you are in sympathy with your hearers they will draw you out to meet their needs.   But avoid any mannerism or tone of voice which may appear to you of specially masculine type, and be perfectly natural and at ease.   The heart of every man is accessible at some point or other, and if a man has been persuaded to come into the church he may be amenable to the power of the Holy Spirit.   Aim at bringing men to Christ, and at bringing them to full communion with the Church and regular attendance at its services.

Preaching to children is one thing.   Catechizing is another   The Prayer Book directs us to do both.   Children are to hear sermons, suitable—one presumes—to their understanding, and the Curate is to catechize on Sundays and Holy Days after the Second Lesson at Evening Prayer.   Sermons to children must of course be simple, but they need not be childish.   Just as much trouble needs to be taken over them as over sermons to adults.   On each occasion try to teach them some definite truth.   But you must keep their interest up all through. Do not attempt to hold their attention by shouting. You will find occasional object sermons of great interest. The Sunday School Institute lends objects of suitable character. But if you invent 'objects' of your own, do not emulate the daring of one of my own colleagues, who sent up a small fire balloon from the pulpit to the delight of the youthful congregation. Needless to say the news of the experiment did not reach me till after the service.

The platform demands gifts of a somewhat different order from those needed in the pulpit. The preacher may not always excel as a platform speaker. But there is no reason why the preacher should not also be a speaker. And whatever the place or the occasion, covet earnestly the best gifts, and seek grace to use them always to the honour and glory of God.

VII.

FEEDING AND TENDING THE FLOCK.

BETWEEN the fulfilment of the bare duties legally necessary to retain a benefice and the fulfilment of the ministry given to a man by our Lord there is a very wide range. Years ago the bare minimum was less than it is to-day. In some cases not even that was observed, and the spiritual torpor prevalent in the Church was aggravated by scandals of pluralism and non-residence and things still worse. The last century has seen the idea of pastoral care rising steadily. It approaches now more nearly the ideal which our Lord in His three-fold charge set before St. Peter : "Feed my Lambs," "Tend my Sheep," "Feed my Sheep" (St. John xxi. 15, 16, 17, R.V.). The collective or corporate and the individualist sides of the clerical office both come into view here. As in pastoral life

so in spiritual, food is to be given to the lambs
and sheep, while individual attention is to be
devoted to those members of the flock which
need it.

We might cite many instances from the
New Testament in which the spiritual food
of the Church is mentioned, but whether the
recipients of the food are young or old,
inexperienced or mature, the food is in one
form or another Christ Himself. The learners
of the A B C of the Faith are said to par-
take of 'milk' (Hebrews v. 12). St. Paul says
(1 Corinthians iii. 2) that he had to keep the
Corinthian Christians longer on 'milk' than he
ought to have done. St. Peter exhorts the
"elect sojourners of the Dispersion" to "long as
newborn babes for the spiritual milk which is
without guile" (1 St. Peter ii. 2, R.V.). For
the Christians of maturer growth 'solid food'
was intended. "Solid food is for full-grown
men, even those who by reason of use have
their senses exercised to discern good and
evil" (Hebrews v. 14, R.V.). The Hebrew
Christians ought to have been on a diet of
solid food, but were not able to bear it. As
to what was intended by 'milk' and 'solid
food' or 'meat,' early commentators supposed
that the 'milk' was teaching on 'our Lord's

humanity,' and that the 'solid food' was the teaching of His Godhead (Westcott on Hebrews v. 12). But, generally speaking, 'milk' corresponds to the foundation principles, and 'solid food' to the more advanced teaching which Christians should assimilate as time went on.

It is ours to supply the food. And specially where preaching or teaching is concerned, the benefits which the recipients of our ministration will derive will depend largely on ourselves. We must be careful to be faithful dispensers of God's Word. "The Bread that I will give is my Flesh, which I will give for the life of the world" (St. John vi. 51). At the same time, the benefit derived from the food will depend partly on the faith of the recipients, and even more upon the sovereign grace of God. In so far as the feeding of the flocks depends on God honouring our ministry, let us be careful that we are not 'hinderers of His Word' or of His grace.

As regards the tending of Christ's sheep, it is difficult to express in words exactly wherein it lies. The pastoral eye, the pastoral heart, and the pastoral lips can only be given and anointed for service by God the Holy Ghost.

o

We must watch for and watch over the souls of our people, as they that must give account—if possible with joy and not with grief. Experience in the use of pastoral gifts will determine the exact method of approach in the case of a particular class or an individual soul. But the best way to exercise these gifts is to enter the ministry at the call of God, constrained by the love of Christ, and in faith that the Holy Spirit has conferred these gifts upon you.

In every fold let us hope that the ninety-and-nine securely lie. In the Parable of the Lost Sheep our Lord represents them as being left for the moment pending the rescue of the lost sheep (St. Luke xv. 4). But He did not imply that they were to be left untended. Our Lord may have meant by the ninety-and-nine to describe with a holy irony the Pharisees. But we are not far wrong in taking them for our purposes to represent the general average of our best Churchpeople, who " need no repentance," and of whom we entertain a good hope. They are by no means to be neglected. We may not assume that because all is well—or apparently well—with them, this state will automatically continue. We must ever seek to keep in touch with them. We must give them of our best. We must be ready to help them in their difficulties, doubts and trials. We must realize that much of our influence is to be exerted through others, and that therefore we must help and train them —perfect them—for *their* work of ministering.

At the same time they ought to be able to walk without crutches and to stand without holding on to our arms. We shall want to bring them into close touch with their Saviour, and to let them draw their strength and support straight from Him, duly using the means of grace which we are permitted to supply to them. If any of them lean too much upon ourselves, we and they must remember that they are preventing us from ministering to someone who may need rescuing, while they themselves are failing to save some soul whom they in turn should reach. So while we do all we can for our ninety-and-nine, it should be with the object of setting their feet upon the Rock and establishing their goings. We should not lavish all—or nearly all—our pastoral care on them, as the manner of some is. We must remember the sheep in the wilderness, and leave the comfortable and easy pastures to seek after them. It may be only one lost sheep, or even a little lamb, but our Lord placed great value upon an individual soul.

Our young men may be numbered among the ninety-and-nine or amongst the 'other' sheep if one may adopt our Lord's expression (see St John x. 16). In any case they require some of our first and best attention. In many parishes they are the special charge of one or more of the assistant clergy. The Vicar's hands are too full of general work to be at once a spiritual father and brother to the young men. But an Assistant-Curate, especially if he be unmarried, can devote himself and his time largely to them. He may approach them in some or all of the following ways : through a Bible-class or guild; through a club or institute; through games; in his own rooms or in their homes. Time must not be grudged to one young man. Late hours must occasionally be kept for his benefit, if he can be approached at no other time. Keep a private register of the young men whom you know, if they are your special charge, and classify them as, for instance, communicants, church-goers, and non worshippers. Do not be content with knowing them well on the cricket-pitch, the football field or in the club. Have some definite spiritual work to draw them to, and at some time or other come to close quarters with each individually. Go over your lists occasionally to see that you have overlooked none, and to ensure that you are doing all that you reasonably can for each. Aim at training them to be true to their Lord in every department of life, and at leading them by various means to be definite workers for God.

Take an interest in their games; play cricket and football with them if you can hold your own and hold your temper; and do not pretend to be a better athlete than you really are. Games have a distinct value in work amongst young men. Having had 'blues' or their equivalent among my own colleagues—one of them appearing twelfth in the averages of last year's first-class batsmen—I am fully alive to the value of athletic prowess. But at the same time we must recognize what games will not effect, and that it is by the Holy Spirit alone that men can be definitely won to God.

Valuable as games are, when put in their right place, we must not under-estimate the importance of literary and debating societies. Some of our young men may become one day candidates for Holy Orders. In any case we shall wish to see them take their places as speakers in the Master's Name, and as members of our local governing bodies. The Church is hardly doing so much as she might do and can do in this direction, and there is often a scarcity of men who can take the lead in holding mission services or speaking in the open air, and of men to nominate for election to our public bodies.

It may seem far-fetched to draw a distinction between lads and young men, but anyone who has had experience of parochial work will understand the difference. The distinction is partly one of age and partly of class. However much one may wish to ignore these distinctions it is impossible to do so. But one can do much to soften asperities and remove ill-feeling. In course of time the utmost friendliness may subsist in a parish between the rougher lads who have been gathered under the wing of the church and the young men who go to the City.

Some one worker may be told off to organize and to superintend a rough lads' club. Do not be in a hurry. In this as in other branches of parish work it is well to let things grow, rather than to force everything into existence all at once. A need will often create a demand, and a demand will lead to a supply, when God's blessing is resting on our work. Here then is room for faith and patience and discernment. To know the right moment, the right thing and the right method will be given to those who ask in faith. At the same time if a club, a society or any other parochial organization is obviously moribund and there is no hope of recovery, it is better to kill it than to let it die. The sixth commandment does not apply in such cases.

But we will anticipate success with your rough lads' class. Call it by some name which will lead the lads to respect the club and to respect themselves. "Victoria Lads' Club" does not sound so bad. See that the superintendent is always on the spot, or adequately represented in his absence. During the holidays of the superintendent of our rough lads' club one summer, the deputy thought that as so few came during the midsummer evenings he need not be present all the time that the club was open. But one evening the lads appeared in force, and finding no one in charge but the bar-keeper, they had a good time and in about twenty minutes did two pounds' worth of damage. The result was that the club had to be closed for two months, after which it was opened with more strictness and greater success. See that the members pay their subscription each week. Allow no arrears. Do not take want of employment as a reason for remitting payment. In such cases suspend use of the club to the member for the time being. Arrange a Bible Class for the members of the Club, and do your best to get them to attend. Where possible let your spiritual influence go further than that. Church, Conversion, Confirmation and Communion are four C's which can be held up as an ideal to the lads. And while spontaneous subscriptions from tradesmen in the neighbourhood and the testimony of the police speak to the value of the work, the sight of some of the lads at church neatly ' clothed and in their right minds ' is more encouraging still. Many of these rough lads will have been at Sunday School, but somehow they have drifted from our influence, and we have to take special pains to recover and reclaim them. Anticipate this difficulty with the present generation of boys. Get them to Sunday School, and keep them there, and when they are too old for Sunday School, provide some bridge spiritual or social to span the gulf which too often divides the clergy from the elder lads of the parish.

By all means place a layman where possible at the head of a Boys' Sunday School. ' The right man' will not only secure efficiency of the teachers, order and affection amongst the boys, but he will find time to further the interests of the School during the week. But if the right man cannot be found, it is better for a Curate to take up the work than to appoint an unsuitable layman. In any parish where boys abound their welfare makes it well worth a Curate's while to undertake this work. In large parishes a secretary may be appointed to assist the superintendent in these duties, though scarcity of teachers may make this difficult. It is not necessary to speak of the Girls' Sunday School, as this will be in the hands of ladies. But do all in your power to foster the work, and shew your interest in both departments by attending when possible to open School.

In some parishes the Sunday School is supplemented or partly superseded by 'the Catechism.' It is becoming fashionable to decry Sunday Schools and to say that their day is done. But they have done splendid work in the past and may do so again. Of course if you are not a believer in the system, you cannot expect it to succeed in your parish. However, if Sunday Schools are in vogue, do your best to uphold your Vicar and to inspire your teachers. The disadvantage of the Catechism is perhaps that it throws more work on the clergy and lessens the scope of the laity. But it is certainly capable of producing excellent results, if no pains be spared to carry out the methods. Some most interesting books on what is known as 'the Catechism' have been edited by Mr. Spencer Jones, and without endorsing his views we can with advantage study his methods, and adapt or reproduce them in our own work. Whatever your methods be, do not grudge giving time or trouble to the work of 'feeding Christ's lambs.' It was the first duty in St. Peter's commission, and it was one-third of the whole. It is ultimately your duty to 'feed' them, and, though you may allow some of the faithful to share this with you as their work of ministering, remember the commission of Him who 'carries the lambs in His bosom,' and love the children and your work amongst them.

I have already spoken about children's services and about catechizing. I might add that we have a morning service for our children at one of our mission churches. The attendance is voluntary, but we have a full church. Possibly the number of children attending may not seem large for a populous parish, but I doubt whether it is wise to make attendance at service immediately after morning school compulsory. A parishioner once told me that he never came to church because when a boy he was compelled to attend thrice a Sunday. He was cut off by early death, without my persuasion meeting with success. Many more perhaps could sincerely, if fallaciously, plead the same excuse.

Your work amongst the 'lambs' will not be limited to Sunday efforts. Teaching in the day schools will be a priceless privilege. After enjoying this opportunity for nearly ten years, how much I missed it on finding in my present parish that the doors of the Church School were closed. Teach in the Church Schools several times a week, if the parish possess schools, and though the benefit to yourself for character, preaching and parochial work cannot be over-estimated, go rather for the sake of the children and their Lord. In another connection I have alluded to this duty (page 186). Here I may add one or two hints. See that the children understand what you teach them. And take care that what they learn by heart they also learn in heart. 'Communion of sins' is a common mistake in saying the Creed in some parts. And I have known a boy make only one mistake in writing out the Lord's Prayer—'but deliver' being replaced by 'bet the liver.' This mistake occurred in a country Board School in Cornwall which I examined for

the Diocesan Inspector.   But Church Schools
have not always clean bills of health in these
respects.   In giving religious instruction remember the position of the Teachers.   You
are not trained to teach ; they are.   And if
the Diocesan Inspector gives a poor report,
the Teachers are likely to receive the blame
unjustly.   And if you do in any way replace
the Teachers in giving instruction, see that
the children do not suffer.

Wherever you are, take every opportunity
of becoming acquainted with the management
of elementary schools, whether provided or non-
provided.   As an Assistant Curate I was on the
management of some twelve Board Schools in
South London.   And when placed in charge
of a parish which had one of the two largest
Church Schools in the diocese, my experience
under the London School Board helped me
in more ways than one.   This kind of experience can only be gained by actual work in a
parish, and it will be of great importance to
begin to learn the details of school management as soon as you are ordained.   Your
first may be your only Curacy.

The subject of day schools must not be left
without mention of pupil-teachers.   They have
before them a position of great influence from a

spiritual point of view. They are at present young and inexperienced, and they will be grateful for your sympathy. They are—at any rate in Church Schools—passing through a period of great strain and pressure, though perhaps not quite so severe as was the case some years ago. And further, their religious instruction is a matter of difficulty if they work in Council Schools, and is not becoming easier under the new arrangements in Church Schools. Do what you can to help them in their religious training. A class may be formed at least for scholarship candidates who are reading for the Archbishops' Examination. That will probably be in the hands of the Vicar. But if it be in your own, be very careful to maintain their self-respect and your own.

One or two adjuncts to work amongst children are of great value. A band or guild in connection with Home or Foreign Missions may do great good—both to the cause of missions and to the members. By all means have Band of Hope work in connection with the Church of England Temperance Society. A branch of the Scripture Union or other society for daily systematic reading of the Bible will be found helpful for training the best of our children in habits of private devotion. It may be well to have a children's evening each week in the parish, arranging a Band of Hope meeting for alternate weeks, and a Scripture Union meeting and a missionary or other meeting once a month each.

Suitable Bible Classes will be arranged to receive the elder children as they pass the Sunday School age—an age which has a different standard in the north from that of the south. Bible Classes for young men and for young women may be arranged in connection with the various clubs and institutes in the parish. But they need not be provided for young people only.

The north of England has shewn us what may be accomplished in this direction. Mr. Swainson, a Holloway Vicar, has lately published a book called *Bible Work and Warfare*, in which he describes the growth of his Sunday Bible Class for men at Sheffield, which after five years reached a membership of 2003, and of his Monday Bible Class for women, which within two years included 1600 members. It may be asked what bearing such classes have upon attendance at Divine Worship and at the Holy Communion, and whether they do not become ends rather than means to an end. In view of such criticism or fear Mr. Swainson's Vicar gives his testimony as to the permanent results of the work in regard to the congregations, Confirmation candidates, communicants, spirituality of Church people, and enthusiasm for the Church. Read the book for yourselves. If you do not carry on a like work or achieve a like success, you will at least be fired with a fresh enthusiasm and will gain confidence as to what can even in these days be done. But whether on a large scale or small, have some kind of Bible Class for your men.

The parable of the Lost Sheep reminds us that the whole of our attention is not to be bestowed on the ninety and nine. Your duty will be not only "to teach, and to premonish, to feed and provide for the Lord's family," but also "to seek for Christ's sheep that are dispersed abroad, and for His children who are in the midst of this naughty world, that they may be saved through Christ for ever." The shepherd—our Lord says—will "go after that which is lost, until he find it" (St. Luke xv. 4).

In like manner the true pastor will devote readily much time and trouble to the seeking and saving of one lost sheep. Every parish has its lost sheep. It may be crime, it may be vice, drunkenness or dishonesty, some social evil, a mania for gambling, which has caused their downfall, or it may be only a disregard for holy things, a forgetting of God, which has marked them with the title 'lost.' For while we associate with the word those whose condition outrages the social conscience, we must remember that in God's sight many who are looked upon as respectable members of society are really lost sheep. It is, however, those who are more obviously lost that call for special tending. Do not be content that they should remain lost; do not give up hope that they can ever be saved. However degraded they may be, shew them that there is something in them which you still respect. Obey the injunction of St. Peter "Honour all men" (1 St. Peter ii. 17).

If you make any impression, follow up the case all the more. And if reformation does not last, do not be disheartened. I heard once of a man in Deptford who was saved from drink ten times before his reclamation was complete. Where drunkenness is concerned personal influence is the best approach. Have your Temperance meetings, and do not fritter away the opportunity which they give.

But the ordinary Temperance meeting will not reclaim drunkards so much as instruct and strengthen young people and others who may be weak and in danger of yielding to temptation. Do not let your Temperance meetings degenerate into mere entertainments. And if they are held less frequently in most parishes than formerly, do not forget to bring the subject forward occasionally at Bible Classes, guilds and mothers' meetings, and also at services in church. Keep a pledge-book going and make use of it in personal work, as well as at the close of a Temperance meeting. But do not urge a drunkard to sign a pledge, if there is little likelihood of his keeping it. His will is gone ; his word will be gone too, if he breaks the pledge. It will be better to let him sign first for a week, then for a month, and so on for longer periods, taking care to keep an eye on him and to renew the pledge, when the period for which he has kept it expires.

Some lost sheep in your parish will owe their downfall to sins of impurity. Some may be more sinned against than sinning. At the same time the guilt of this sin must never be minimised. Where you know a man to be a profligate, you can speak faithfully to

P

him of his sin. But dealing with such case
often requires special tact and experience, an
it is generally best for you to report such case
to your Vicar, and leave him to deal with ther
personally or to give you his instruction
Where the sinner or the victim is a woma
or young girl, caution is doubly necessary
In such cases report at once to the Vica
He will probably place the case in the hand
of a rescue worker, who will be able to dra
the young woman to a rescue home, or to
penitentiary, as may prove desirable. If yo
suspect any girls to be in moral danger, d
not lose time in reporting the matter.
you fear that any girl is placing herself i
the way of temptation, tell the Vicar, an
he through the rescue worker will be abl
to send her to a preventive home. Do no
scent evil where evil is not, and do not suspe
wrong without real reason. At the same tim
do not be alarmed at the appearance of tar
among the wheat. Keep your conscienc
tender on the subject of this sin, and whe
you do come in contact with it remembe
the difficulty of touching pitch without bein
defiled. Watch over your young men an
boys, encourage them in what is pure, forti
them against temptation, foster a healthy ton

nd shew them that the strength of Christ is he only means by which they can hope to vercome. Whatever be the sin which has aused one here and another there to become lost sheep, do not be content with half neasures. The only security against falling gain is to be in Christ. "If any man be in Christ, he is a new creature" (2 Corinthians . 17).

A very useful purpose in tending the sheep vill be served by prayer-meetings. These may be general for the whole parish, or limited to one centre or branch of parochial work. There s in some quarters a tendency to despise or to overlook the importance of a prayer-meeting. But a prayer-meeting is at least as helpful n the working of a parish as a parish magazine. And few clergymen find that they can dispense with so useful an adjunct of their work as a parish magazine. An interesting pamphlet entitled *Prayer-Meetings for Churchmen: a Practical Guide to their Management*, has lately been issued by the S.P.C.K. It is written by Mr. Harris, one of the Lecturers at Lampeter, and Examining Chaplain to the late Bishop of Llandaff. As the writer is a Priest Associate of the Confraternity of the Blessed Sacrament, he will not be suspected

of any bias when he writes: "The onl
religious movement of recent times whic
has neglected prayer meetings is the Oxfor
movement. . . . This attitude of the High
Church party as a whole towards prayer
meetings is to be regretted, because it deprive
them of one of the most potent means ye
devised of evangelizing the masses and kind
ling religious enthusiasm." Father Dolling
must have shared Mr. Harris' opinion, as in
his work at Landport he gave scope to his
people to offer extempore prayer for one
another's needs and for the work of the
Church.

Year by year in a parish of any size
candidates will be presented to the Bishop for
Confirmation. In one sense preparation for
this rite will always be going on, and the
clergy should always be on the watch for
candidates, and should bring the matter before
likely persons, thus giving them ample time
for consideration of the question before the
actual preparation begins. Such names will
be noted in a book, and will be gone over
when the lists of candidates are compiled just
prior to the preparation. Notice should be
given in church and in the parish magazine,
and every house in the parish should be visited

and a letter with notice giving particulars of the classes should be left. The classes should be preceded by a gathering of all the likely candidates in the parish church, perhaps on a Sunday evening, when the subject can be introduced by an instruction from the Vicar. The classes—perhaps many in number—will meet once each week for two months, conducted by the more experienced of the parochial clergy. They should begin and end punctually, especially if they are for female candidates. During these weeks the subjects treated lead up to the Confirmation, and that alone. After the Confirmation the classes should be continued for a month, and instruction on the Holy Communion should be given. The work should then be completed by a First Communion for the candidates on a particular Sunday. As regards the candidates, do not encourage them to come forward at too early an age. Bishop Gott used to prescribe 14 years as the lowest age in the Diocese of Truro. Out of more than six hundred candidates whom I have presented in the last few years only one has been below that age, and though others may take a different view my experience does not allow me to find such restriction a hardship. Encourage adults to come forward. Amongst my male candidates last year were ten men brought to me by the Senior Curate.

Induce anyone who is open to conviction to attend the classes, but weed out your candidates. The requirements of the rite will have that effect as the classes proceed. You want numbers, but quality must come first. Have a private interview with each, and press upon each the necessity of decision for Christ before being able to give the answer, "I do," to the solemn question of the Bishop. Note down each year any points on which you want to speak privately to the candidates. Do not crowd too much on them at a private interview, but some of the following points may be touched upon: decision for Christ; private prayers; knowledge of Catechism; reading of Bible; regularity at Holy Communion; interest in Missions; definite work for God. Various subjects may be taken at the Classes. The late Bishop Wynne published a helpful little volume called *Our Confirmation Class* some years ago, and the late Canon Robinson, Rector of Whitechapel and afterwards Rector of Birmingham, published an excellent outline of Confirmation addresses. There are other similar volumes. My own practice is to expound the teaching of Scripture on the Laying on of hands; then to go through the subjects suggested by the Confirmation Service, dwelling particularly on the promises included in the Baptismal vow, the need of continuance in the Christian life, and the nature of the blessing which we may expect from God at Confirmation; closing the list with an address on the subject of private prayer.

One may be tempted to get so much as possible into the golden period of preparation, but it is a temptation to be resisted, and I doubt the wisdom of setting papers of questions for the candidates to answer week by week. Some have not the time, others have not the education, and others have not the confidence, to write their answers with any satisfaction to themselves. After the classes have dispersed, enrol the candidates in one or other of your communicants' classes, and enter them in your roll of communicants.

This list will be very useful to you in tending the sheep. You will by keeping it up to date learn of the lapse of any communicants. And though attendance at Holy Communion is not by any means the one criterion of spiritual life, neglect of the rite nearly always betokens a decline in the life of the soul. Arrange your communicants according to roads. Keep two lists of roads in alphabetical order, one for the roads in your parish or district, the other for the roads outside in which communicants under your charge may reside. Each road should be given sufficient space for a list of male communicants who live in that road, and then for a list of female, leaving room for future names to be added. You will find this mode of classification very useful for sending out circular letters and notices to your communicants. The envelopes will be sorted as they are addressed. You will also find it useful for purposes of visitation. A list of communicants in a particular road is ready for you at a moment's notice. Keep your roll as carefully as possible, noting the correct address in cases of removal. Enter up your roll after the celebration, doing so from memory. Do not be afraid of missing a few names. All you need to do is to get an idea as to which communicants are drawing away or growing cold. And if you scan too carefully the faces of those who communicate, your mind may be distracted and you may forget to breathe that prayer over each communicant for which so happy an opportunity is given.

Thus and in other ways you will tend and

feed the Church of God, which He has purchased with His own Blood. While you do so, beware of the grievous wolves which enter in among you, not sparing the flock. The true pastor will shew himself to be such by his attitude in the face of dangers to his people. "But he that is an hireling, . . . whose own the sheep are not, seeth the wolf coming, and leaveth the sheep, and fleeth" (St. John x. 12). There are many enemies of the flock of Christ against whom we have to guard our people and ourselves, but the warning which I wish to emphasize is against professed friends— wolves in sheep's clothing. "Of your own selves shall men arise" (Acts xx. 30). Others there still are in the flock of Christ, "of whom," says St. Paul, "I have told you often, and now tell you even weeping, that they are the enemies of the Cross of Christ ; whose end is destruction, whose god is their belly, and whose glory is in their shame, who mind earthly things" (Philippians iii. 18, 19). Thieves and robbers attack the Church of Christ. We shall look out for them. But we must take heed to ourselves. Our conduct and our motives will need watching all the time.

It was said of one earnest country clergyman— one by no means unfriendly to Nonconformists,

" Nonconformity could not lift up its head in W——. The parishioners found all they needed in the ministry of the parish church." Provide all the food possible for your people. See that when the hungry sheep look up they are duly fed. And if you are faithful to your trust, you may be sure that God who only giveth the increase will give you your reward and will not send the people empty away.

VIII.

THE PASTOR AS A VISITOR.

" I AM not a believer in house-to-house visitation." Such is the convenient verdict of
ignorance which is sometimes pleaded in
justification of neglect of duty. An airy
excuse like this may prove a dangerous in-
dulgence. For, quite apart from the common
sense of the saying, " a house-going parson
makes a church-going people," the Church
prescribes this as one of the few plain duties
which devolve upon the Deacon. " It is his
Office, where provision is so made, to search
for the sick, poor and impotent people of the
Parish, to intimate their estates, names and
places where they dwell, unto the Curate that
by his exhortation they may be relieved with
the alms of the Parishioners, or others."
How after that a Deacon can enlarge upon
his views as to house-to-house visitation, it is

difficult to see. The Church does not invite him to state his views, still less to modify his conduct according to them. She says to him, There is your parish, go and visit the people. She asks, "Will you do this gladly and willingly?" He replies, "I will so do, by the help of God."

The next day he goes from the Bishop's house to his parish. And after a day or so for settling in, he is taken down to a particular district by his Vicar. The lie of the parish is explained to him, and the Vicar then conducts him through the eight, ten or twelve streets which comprise the Curate's 'district.' There will be some centre of work in the shape of a mission or a schoolroom, or a club to which he can draw the people, and from which his influence will radiate. Or the district may be worked in connection with a mission in an ad-joining district, or with the parish church. The various landmarks—public-houses, for instance —objects of interest and centres of evil and good will be pointed out to the new Curate, and some of the homes where he will find friends or foes are shewn to him. Then he pays his first visit. The Vicar takes him to a few houses, one or two where he will find loyal supporters; one or two more where there are invalids who will welcome his regular ministrations ; and perhaps one or two where drink or squalor range themselves in opposition to Christ. The first afternoon in the district will soon end, and the Curate will be formally installed.

The task of visiting street after street and getting to know the people may appear formidable enough, but he now knows that not every door will be shut against him, and that God has at least some people in that district. Before we tackle the actual work, we must give our friends the Priests a turn. I have been speaking of house-to-house visiting as a duty specially incumbent on Deacons. And in the Ordinal there is less explicit mention of this work as being enjoined on Priests. It may be that the Priest is considered to have come to years of clerical discretion, and to be confirmed in his office by the laying on of the hands of the presbytery, and that therefore he does not need quite so plain directions on the subject of pastoral visitation. But is not the framing of these instructions the fruit of generations of the Church's experience ? A Deacon is beginning his work. The ground is virgin soil, so far as he is concerned. He may inherit most useful information from his predecessor in the Curacy, if there has been one, and if his work has been faithful. But in any case he has to make the acquaintance of the people afresh. And this requires constant drudgery for some months at least, if not for the year or more of his diaconate. As he becomes acquainted with his people, he finds that some more than others need his help, some cases (the word is useful, though rather odious) require following up, and his visiting becomes more and more special. By the time he is ordained Priest the larger part of his time is taken up by special cases, and the commission now entrusted to him is of a more general character, "to use both publick and private monitions and exhortations, as well to the sick as to the whole, within your Cures, as need shall require, and occasion shall be given." But the Priest still believes in house-to-house visitation and does what he can, not only to keep his hand in, but more, to seek to reach *all* the people entrusted to his charge.

At the outset of his work the Deacon should provide himself with a large note-book as a register of his district. Each street should be entered and indexed, and four or five lines of a fairly wide page should be

allowed for every house. Ideally there ought
to be in a town parish some 2000 people
under the charge of the Deacon. They would
comprise some 400 families, and would require
about 2000 lines in the register. Room is
thereby left for entering the developments of
family history, and for noting the names of
the new families which will be constantly
coming into the parish. In advocating the
use of such a book one is treading on
dangerous ground. Canon Savage, in his
Pastoral Visitation, deprecates more than the
keeping of a visiting note-book to enter the
names of the families, "and a few perfectly
general and harmless facts about them." But
writing in another volume[1] in the same series,
Mr. Clement Rogers advises, for purposes of
relief at least, the entry of the most circumstantial details in books or on cards. Combining the advice of the two writers, we may
deduce that at any rate some book must be
kept; that the utmost care is necessary as to
what is written down, though the notes must
be more than 'general and harmless facts';
and that the book must be kept from the
eyes of others. Certainly anything salient
having regard to the winning of one soul to

[1] *Charitable Relief* (Handbooks for the Clergy.
Longmans, Green & Co.).

God may be entered in the book, and any information bearing on the character or needs of families likely to come within range of relief should be noted. These notes might be entered in shorthand if you are a master of the art, for the sake of privacy and of space in your book. But see that your shorthand does not become untranslatable a few weeks after it is written.

The information thus recorded you will find most useful when application is made to you as to the character of various people who may have been in your district. Last week I received a letter from a former Curate asking me to attend to the needs of a parishioner who had written in piteous terms for help. Of course it was the first time he had ever asked for aid. Something in the handwriting made me think I had come across the man when living at another address. On looking up the name I found that two years ago one of the Bishops had been troubled by the same gentleman, on the plea of wishing to lead a new life on release from gaol, and that inquiries made by me on behalf of the Bishop had shewn that the man was utterly untrustworthy. The man has since justified my description by incurring a sentence of some months' duration. But whatever notes you make, write nothing down in the house when you visit, and tell any new district visitors to avoid the same mistake.

It will be well to keep a second book. Enter in your journal or pocket-book the names and addresses of all whom you visit. This may sound burdensome, but if you do it every day it will not take many minutes. Do not fail to make your entries at least every week, or the completeness and value of the book will be gone. This plan has the advantage of helping you to keep up your weekly average, and to watch over the expenditure of your time. Each day's opportunities can thus be reviewed, with the use made of them. Note the number of hours which you spend in actual visiting each day. The loss of time in the course of an afternoon's work may be more than you realize. The number of visits in the course of a week will vary according to the parish, but in an average town parish a Curate ought to visit for some fifteen hours in the week at least. If he is visiting from house to house he will cover the ground more quickly, and in the course of a week may pay some fifty or sixty visits. But as time goes on his attention will be more occupied with special cases, and the total will fall lower. This does

not mean that his work will be of less value
it may be of more.   We must beware of sacri
ficing thoroughness to numbers.   At the same
time if the numbers are scanty, the visitor is
at fault, and taking a long visit with a shor
one, perhaps a door-step visit, the average i
fairly maintained.   Canon Savage estimate
that a Vicar should accomplish some thirty
pastoral visits in a week ; Bishop Chavass
says that twenty-five should be taken as
minimum.   But remember that a Curate—and
specially a Deacon—ought to shew a mucl
larger record of visits than a Vicar.   And d
not be content with a certain number of hour
in the district or a respectable total of visit
on a particular day.   You are sent to ministe
to all the souls in your district and to win al
you can to the side of Christ.   Never b
satisfied with what you have been able to do

Before you go out write a list of th
people whom you have to visit specially, o
look through your book with the cases whic
you have on hand.   There are three suppose
failings in connection with visiting, which w
are inclined to excuse in ourselves—ignorance
overlooking, and forgetting.   For the firs
there is some excuse.   We cannot know auto
matically who is ill or in trouble in the parisl

At the same time if we are in close touch with the people, and if we are assiduous in house-to-house visiting, we shall hear of many cases which need attention in a way that would otherwise be impossible. For overlooking cases there is very little excuse, and for forgetfulness no excuse whatever is allowable. Never forget a sick case. It is your business to remember. Laziness is the real fault in the matter. These failings can be guarded against by keeping memoranda of the persons whom it is well to visit regularly or occasionally. Before you start ask God's blessing on your afternoon's work, that you may redeem the opportunities; that you may be faithful in testimony; that you may have the love of Christ in your heart; and that you may exhibit the gift of sympathy. If you come from the presence of God, the presence of God will go with you into the homes of your people. It was said of a country clergyman who was cut off in his prime, " His bed in the afternoon bore the impression continually of where his praying form had knelt before he went out to visit." Start out always early in the afternoon.

The sick will have the first claim on your attention. Some of these may be chronic cases, requiring a visit once a week or twice

a month. In these cases go so far as possible
on a fixed day, and about the same time of the
day. Cases of ordinary sickness may require
visiting once, twice or thrice weekly, or even
daily. Much depends upon the particular case.
And it is impossible to lay down any rule.
Your own judgment guided by the Holy Spirit
must decide what is desirable. Do not go
merely because duty calls you. And when
you are at the house bear in mind two things,
that you are there for the good of the patient
and for the glory of God. You will speak
softly and move gently in a house where sickness prevails. Do not be long in the sick
room. And do not press the patient to talk.
If he wishes to do so, let him. It may be a
relief. But you will generally know. Incessant questions however are generally a
trouble. You have in view the recovery of
the patient, and his introduction to God or his
strengthening in the faith. Sympathy may
lead you to gloss over the sins of a past life
and it may seem cruel to a patient struggling
with death to hint that all may not be well
with the soul, yet you have before all things
to be faithful.

Death-bed repentance may not always be
sincere, as is shewn by cases when recovery

has unexpectedly occurred. But it must never-
theless be aimed at where there is no evidence
of previous repentance.

Do not in any way usurp the functions of
doctor or nurse. And do not let it be supposed
that your entrance into the sick room is the
harbinger of death. Be bright and cheery if
grave and solemn. Sing to the patient, if your
voice and the patient's condition permit. Do
not take exception to the presence of friends or
relations in the sick room. Read or repeat a
few verses of Scripture, and do not forget to
pray. In some cases it will be well to ask
the patient whether he would like you to
specially mention any wish of his own in your
prayer. Pray extempore, though occasionally
in chronic cases a prayer from the Prayer
Book or a devotional manual may be useful.
You will perhaps never use the office for the
Visitation of the Sick in its entirety, but some
of it you will find useful from time to time,
especially the exhortation to the sick person.

You will after your ordination as Priest be
able from time to time to administer the Holy
Communion to the sick. At all times such a
service is solemn, but specially so when it is
obvious that a few weeks or even days must
break earthly communion with the sufferer.

Be punctual always in the case of an appointed visit, and even if the patient expects you at a time of which you are aware, though you have made no promise to come. But be doubly careful to attend punctually for the Communion of the Sick. Remember the three preliminary conditions : (1) at least two to communicate with the sick person ; (2) a convenient place ; (3) all things necessary prepared for reverent ministration. Do not consider any tenement too squalid to administer the sacrament in. Remember that our Lord was laid at His Birth in a manger, and at His Death hung on a cross.

The sacrament of Baptism will be occasionally administered privately to sick children. In such cases try to give at the time some hints as to the nature of the rite, and perhaps later on—if the child lives—fuller instruction as to the privileges and responsibilities associated with Baptism. Explain also the identity of the rite as administered privately with Public Baptism at the parish church. Ill-instructed parents sometimes wish to bring their children to be baptized a second time. Explain in such cases the meaning of the service for reception into the Church, and invite them to avail themselves of it. Be careful to write down the particulars needed for the register, and do not forget to enter them afterwards.

Where prolongation of life is a mercy, we can pray throughout that the Lord will heal the sick, and we can believe in His power to do so even when human aid can do no more. But in some cases death is the termination of illness. We may especially in the early days of ministry make mistakes as to the issue of illness in certain cases. We may go to one house half fearing that the patient will be gone, and find that a turn for the better has taken place. We may go to another thinking quite lightly of the patient's physical condition and find that death has already taken place. A clergyman once visited a patient in the Bristol Infirmary. He thought that he would have at least one more opportunity of seeing the sick man. So he spoke to him specially of the guilt of sin in a man's life, intending to point him to the Saviour the next day. But on the following day the man was dead, and only half the message had been given.

We need wisdom at all times to speak a word in season, but above all when death seems near. Then our words must come from our hearts if they are to help the dying man. Then above all other times we shall find how necessary it is to be prepared by continual communion with God to speak naturally the language of heaven. If desired by the dying man or his friends be willing to stay in the room so long as you can be of service. And when the moment of departure comes, commend in prayer the departing spirit to God.

When death occurs in a family do all you can to minister to the bereaved. Visit them as may be helpful to them before the burial. Do not expect to be always invited indoors at such times. Some families prefer to be let alone, others seem to cling to all the human help they can get. You may or may not be asked to officiate at the burial. If the burials of the parish take place in a cemetery at some distance, you will find that constant attendance makes a considerable demand upon your time. But if asked to attend, do not decline unless obliged. And after the burial, do not entirely overlook the family in pastoral ministration.

Encourage your people to send for you in case of sickness. Be always at their disposal in such cases. The paralysed man described in St. Mark's Gospel (ii. 1 to 12) was healed for the faith of those who bore him and let him down through the roof into the house where our Lord was. And those who send for you may be as the bearers who carry their sick one into the presence of Jesus for healing.

Last autumn a young widow of about twenty-two years of age called on me one morning to visit her cousin who was dying of consumption. The poor girl had left home at seven o'clock and had walked four miles in the wet and cold, with bad boots and no breakfast, to secure ministration for her cousin. And when I offered her breakfast she preferred to take me to see the sick girl at once and to come back for some breakfast afterwards. At evening the cousin died, but surely her friend's faith in her behalf met with due reward.

Go at once in such cases if you learn from your informant that your presence is immediately desired. In cases where private baptism is desired, lose not a moment.

In visiting the whole you will go from house to house, and you will visit special cases. These will include communicants; Church workers; members of Bible Classes and various organizations connected with the Church; persons whom you have seen at Church, or whom you have had succeeded in influencing to some extent, or whom you wish to aid. As time goes on you will find these special cases increase in number and absorb more of your time. Do not go too often to or lavish too much time on particular houses, which you happen to be fond of visiting. In these cases you will generally be asked indoors. But whether you are invited to enter or not, remember to observe the most elementary rules of courtesy. Do not be too inquisitive. You do not go to the house to find out all about the family's circumstances, but to lead them to God. At the same time where you are natural and sympathetic, little things will come out which will throw light on the situation, and things which you want to know will be elicited by the exercise of a little tact. Only it is not tact to ask a question indirectly in such a way that your real purpose is only too obvious. It is far better to ask a question straight out than to do that.

In house-to-house visiting you will often at your first call be accorded an interview on the door-step. Do not mind this. Guard against taking cold in the winter, as you go from house to house. But do not grudge any discomfort on other grounds. Visit in the evenings or on Saturday afternoons when possible. You will then be more likely to see the men, for the drawback of afternoon visiting is that in visiting the whole one finds few men at home. But with the increasing organization of labour in great concerns like railways, the postal service and the police force, the hours of the workers are being adjusted in such a way that employés are in many cases at home for some part of the day during certain weeks.

The fact however that in two cases out of three you will see the woman of the house in house-to-house visiting during the afternoon need not cause you to undervalue the efficacy of your work. Your visit and probably your words will be duly reported to the husband when he comes home, and if your words have been wise good may be done indirectly as well as directly. And after all Christianity is a religion for the home, and the influence of woman in home life is paramount. At an important meeting held last autumn in Westminster to promote the training of nurses one of our leading physicians said that the mothers of England were the most valuable lives that the nation possessed. So make use of your opportunities : remember that on the mothers the burden of the home chiefly falls, and in times of sickness or want of employment the strain must become almost intolerable. They need the help of God to carry out their home duties and to train their children for God, and a word or two spoken in sympathy may lead not only one soul but a whole family to look up to God. Think beforehand what to say, especially if you know who will open the door. Prepare your message to the individual man or woman if not as carefully and as precisely, at least as surely and as regularly as you prepare to speak to the congregation in church. And when emergency calls for an unprepared message, you may feel sure that it will be given you what you shall speak.

Do not be discouraged by apparent rebuffs. Three weeks after my ordination a railway porter opened the door of a house in response to my knock. Seeing me he bluntly remarked, "We don't require the acquaintance of the Church here," and then he slammed the door in my face. My desire to be of some use to him received a rude check, and I almost dreaded to knock at a door again. However as during the whole of my subsequent experience I have never met with a similar reception, it has since occurred to me that something in my manner or bearing may have roused the parishioner's ire on that occasion.

As you go through your district aim at being thorough in your work. There may be two or three families living in one house, and having seen the mother of one you may imagine that she represents the whole household. In a courteous manner you can find out what other families live in the house, and whether there are any lodgers. Do not forget to visit the tradesmen in your district, and be on the lookout for the spiritual welfare of shop assistants. In newer districts the practice of building workmen's flats is on the increase. In my own neighbourhood not only have hundreds of such flats been built, but many houses of older construction have been divided into flats. This has the effect of making visiting somewhat easier, and it also ensures to each family more of that privacy which is essential to the fostering of healthy home life.

In any case a little civility goes a long way. In the parish where I was Curate a working man on whom I called invited me to tea. He happened to have some friends with him who were spending a holiday in London. We became very friendly, but soon parted, and there the matter ended, as one supposed. But three years later on my appointment to a parish over 300 miles distant I found that my two friends were parishioners of my new parish. When

they found who their new Vicar was they
spread a good report in the poor part of the
parish, which was of the utmost service to me
in taking up the work. Every word we say
may be a seed—for good or for evil. And in
moments of discouragement about our work in
our district we may reflect that what we have
tried to do may be fraught with good results in
distant times and places, or perhaps earlier and
nearer home.

Our very words are important and the
question suggests itself as to what is to be
our procedure in pastoral visitation, when we
are admitted into a house. How far is religion
to come in? or to be dragged in? In this as
in other ministrations it may not be dragged in.
It must come in as part of ourselves. It may
not be left outside because it cannot be left
outside. But more than that, if we really
believe in the Holy Ghost, we may be sure
that He who has sent us to the house will
enter it with us. So much having been said,
we must remember that we enter to win the
members of that family to God. But we do
not wish to take them out of the world.
Religion is to enter their home on the plane of
their home life. So we must be quite natural
and take the utmost interest in the life of the

home. Christ entered into home life and
sanctified it. But we must not stop there. It
might be urged that if we were to be perfectly
natural we should probably enter many homes
without speaking directly on religion. If that
were true, it might bespeak a low standard
in our own religious character. But after all
we enter these homes with a definite message
from God. Are we faithful if we go away
without giving it? What would the landlord
say if his rent-collector called and left after a
pleasant conversation without saying a word
about the rent? The parallel is not quite
exact, but the criticism holds good. You go to
a house on your heavenly Father's business and
whether welcome or not, that business must be
transacted. There are times when it is possible
to say more than at others. There are times
when very little can be said, as for instance
when the house is full of friends. But generally
something can be said to bring the hearer face
to face with God. When opportunity offers,
a few verses from God's Word can be read
and their bearing on the lives of your hearers
can be explained. I doubt whether this is so
usual in pastoral visitation as was once the
case. Some years ago a Vicar in a country
parish advertized for a Curate who would 'visit

the people with the Word of God.'   Was not
this the true ideal ?

In most houses which we enter it will be
possible to offer prayer.   In visiting sick
people you will almost invariably close your
visit with prayer.   And in visiting the whole
you should make this a frequent practice.
You will of course always ask the permission
of the head of the house to offer prayer.   Such
permission will not often be refused.   This
rule applies in any house where you are in
spiritual charge of the family, whatever be their
social standing.   And this may be said of the
working classes, in spite of their alleged
estrangement from religion—they are often
more appreciative of prayer by a clergyman
in their homes than are families connected
with the upper classes.   But even in houses
where prayer is not likely to be welcome,
give the opportunity and accept the situation
if the offer be declined.   Once when a new
row of villas had been erected I called in due
course on the occupant of the first—a widow
of middle age.   She gave me permission to
offer prayer for blessing on her new home.
Some time afterwards I learned that though
she attended a church in a neighbouring
parish she was very much hurt at my

asking to offer prayer, and remarked that I was not likely to pray in a house of the R——s, naming the leading family in the neighbourhood. Even so, none of the family named were parishioners, and as a matter of fact I had, not long previously, at the wish of the family, offered prayer in one of the houses named.

With the spiritual results of our action on such occasions we are not concerned. It is ours to be instant out of season as well as in season. And at best we shall be more likely to err in not fulfilling our duty than in exceeding it. The results must be left to God. The danger most to be guarded against is lest our conduct at such times may seem to be inconsistent with our known spiritual character. And, more often than we suppose, our failure to leave some spiritual impression will be noticed and criticized, even in homes where little religion is affected. See that what people expect of you is at least realized. If you do go beyond that, do not feel troubled. In things spiritual, it is yours to lead ; the people are to follow. And if you feel the want of a word of encouragement from those whom you visit, which would help you to minister to them,

R

remember that they may feel the same need of encouragement from you and be more shy to open out, while you are teacher and they are learners. Whatever you do, remember in pastoral visitation the aim set before you in the Ordinal—"that there be no place left among you, either for error in religion, or for viciousness in life."

In a large parish you will nearly always have some of your people in hospitals. Their spiritual interests will probably be looked after there, but do what you can to help them with your own ministrations. As a rule you will not be able to visit a hospital patient more than once a week, though special circumstances may demand more frequent attention. But go when you can and on days when the friends of the patient are not admitted. You will then have the patient's whole attention, and your visit will be the more welcome, as it will lessen the intervals between the visits of friends. The sight of someone from home is always agreeable to a hospital patient, and however efficient and sympathetic the Chaplain may be, it will be easier for the patient to speak more freely to his own clergyman. Always ask permission of the Sister before entering the ward. Do not mind waiting some time if the physician or surgeon is in the ward. And do not stay too long, especially if the patient be very weak after an operation. Speak in an undertone, but make your patient hear without an effort. As a rule kneel down and pray with your parishioner before going from the ward, and leave some thought expressed in the form of a text from Scripture. If you promise to come again, keep your promise. As you pass out of the ward, a nod or a word to some of the patients may give them pleasure. You will be able to tell when this will be acceptable. If you see the Sister on leaving the ward, thank her for admitting you. Then get back to your district as soon as possible.

There may be a hospital in your own parish. If your Vicar be Chaplain, take full advantage of the opportunity of ministering there. The experience will be useful to you, but go for a higher motive than that—to be of some use to the staff and patients. In any case see that you commend your religion by your brightness and sympathy.

Possibly the isolation hospital for the district may be in your own parish. Generally speaking isolation hospitals are more likely to be devoid of pastoral ministration than other hospitals. This is not so much owing to the infectious nature of the diseases treated there, as to the fact that hospitals of this nature are managed by the local authorities and supported out of the rates, and the disposition not to assign Church of England Chaplains to institutions under such control is growing. In the London fever hospitals accredited Chaplains are always at work.

However if there be no special Chaplain, your Vicar will probably undertake the duties, or at any rate pay some attention to the spiritual needs of the patients and staff. Do not be afraid of the danger of infection. For nearly four years I have had charge of an isolation hospital with four wards. During that time I have never known anyone officially connected with the hospital contract any of the complaints treated there, except in the case of a domestic servant in the matron's house, who took scarlet fever in a mild form. And you will not run the same risk as is incurred by the medical and nursing staff. At the same time some risk must be incurred. Eleven years ago a South London Vicar was Chaplain of a large fever hospital in his parish. After working there without harm for

two and a half years he contracted scarlet
fever in a severe form and though young and
robust succumbed after four days' illness. It
is therefore idle to pretend that there is
absolutely no risk. But the risk will be
almost as great for others as for yourself.
Take therefore all proper precautions. Go to
the hospital soon after a good meal. Wear
a cassock which will envelope you from chin
to foot. Wash your hands and face on leaving.
Have a good airing, not forgetting to bare
your head, before you enter any other house.
And do not visit a sick case directly after
visiting the isolation hospital.

The workhouse or the infirmary may be
in your parish. In any case you will have
parishioners in both—in some cases perma-
nently, in others temporarily. Do not forget
either. Those who for the time being are
nursed in the infirmary you will visit in the
same way as parishioners who are in-patients
at hospitals. Even those who are there for
life must not be forgotten. There will be
little enough to remind them of the world
which they have so reluctantly left. Do not
forget to send them a little gift at Christmas,
and go to see them when you can. If any
of them are communicants, send them copies

of notices which you may be sending at any time to the communicants of your parish.

At all times keep your Vicar informed of any special cases in your district which may need his attention. "Intimate"—as the Ordinal directs—full particulars, and keep him in touch with the people in your district. He may not know many of them personally, but by judicious assistance from yourself he will be able to know the names and more of many of your people. Do not be afraid to ask his advice as to how to deal with cases of particular difficulty. And tell him of any spiritual encouragement which you receive. Do not shrink from shewing him your visiting books, but welcome every inquiry from him as to the progress of your work. You will be of course his colleague in the ministry, and before long you will be advanced to the same order as he holds. At the same time he is responsible for the souls of all the parishioners, and he will pay you to do work which he cannot do himself, and it is due to him to know how that work is progressing. Look upon any account which you may be asked to give him not as an inquisitorial interference with your liberty, but as a mark of interest in your work and of a desire to help you. It will soon be

evident from the tenour of his remarks that
such is really his wish.   And do not resent
an occasional criticism or rebuke, if there is
any indication of slackness on your part.

Be careful moreover not to judge the visiting
which you suppose the Vicar to do or not to
do by your own standard.   Your duties are
simple and definite.   He has numerous other
duties of which you know little and realize
less.   If he visits little, be the more careful
to "intimate" to him the names, addresses
and circumstances of "the sick, poor and
impotent people of the Parish."   And if
you read in the biography of a parish priest
of great reputation that he "was never at
any period of his ministry a house-to-house
visitor," do not lay to your soul the flattering
unction that you are excused by circumstances
of a similar kind.   Remember that the biographer of the same clergyman continues,
"It was not possible for him to be so [*i.e.*
a house-to-house visitor] consistently with the
enormous calls upon his time for other
necessary purposes. . . .   As he never visited
any except special cases (and of course always
including sick beds, where his ministry was
perfect in its tact and tenderness), he was
forced to rely very largely on the efforts of

his staff . . . seeing the people in their own homes—on which he laid the very greatest importance. . . . He knew however the details of every case. . . . Besides this, a great part of every day was devoted to 'seeing people,' as he called it" (*Life of Dolling*, Osborne, p. 77).

You will find much help in your work, especially if your district be large, from the co-operation of lady district visitors. For influencing the life of the home such workers are invaluable. But the difficulty is to find or to train women of suitable gifts to undertake this work. And in large and poor parishes it is often more difficult to find women who have sufficient leisure for this purpose. However, do what you can to help and to be helped by your district visitors. Set a few to work, if you cannot get many. And even if they can do only a little, that, well done, is better than none at all. In some parishes men are set to work to visit the men in particular streets, specially in connection with the Men's Service or Bible Class. Such work if systematically done is invaluable. In any case see that the men are not neglected in the daily ministration.

In pastoral visitation experience will be the

best teacher—perhaps more so than in any other branch of your work. You may feel a shrinking from facing it, and this reluctance may cling to you after years of work. But do not give way to it. Start out day by day at the appointed hour, fulfil daily your tale of bricks, and you will find that no part of your work will give you greater cause for thankfulness and that no part will yield better results.

IX.

THE PASTOR AS A MAN OF METHOD.

WHAT a dreadful word in connection with Church work is Organization. One almost shudders when one hears that Mr. So-and-so is a very good organizer. Visions of red tape and of unspirituality rise up before the mind. We think of men who make a business of their spiritual calling, and little else. And we are at times tempted to revolt from the idea of careful organization in our desire to exalt the spiritual side of our office. It has been increasingly felt of late that excessive attention is being paid to details of parochial and ecclesiastical organization, and that spiritual life and spiritual force are suffering. Church life may be vigorous, but the life of the Church is less healthy than of old. The *Guardian* summed this up in a leading article last August on the subject of "Organization and Spiritual Force." It stated that many people are more ready to give time and energy to attending at meetings or committees than to engaging in directly spiritual work or to maintaining their own spiritual fervour. "But if the spiritual fervour be lacking, the organization will not continue for long to discharge its work efficiently. For a time the machinery may run by itself, and the men who have formed the habit of attending public meetings or of sitting on committees may themselves continue to give their services. But they will not make any converts or leave successors to take their places, nor will their work be of the same quality as if there were greater spiritual force behind it." There is much truth in these words. One sometimes goes to a parochial, ruri-decanal or diocesan conference or committee, hoping to return to work with fresh enthusiasm and zeal, and one returns too often with a sense of having accomplished very little in the way of actual business, and perhaps with the feeling of having caught a spiritual chill. It may be one's own fault, but the impression remains.

At the same time careful organization is of great importance. The clergy are credited by the world with not being men of business. Their reputation accordingly suffers and their words are discounted by business men. In some quarters this notion is carried further— the clergy are charged with being bad administrators of parochial finance, and that is made an excuse for withholding contributions for church purposes. In extreme cases the notion goes further still, and ill-disposed persons are ready to imagine that in default of exact and accurate balance-sheets the clergy may in such cases be allowing money given for church objects to find its way into their own pockets. All this may seem very absurd, but we have to face all kinds of prejudices which are only too readily entertained by men who will make of anything an excuse for rejecting the message of revelation.

Careful organization is also important in these days of high pressure because it enables one to cover more ground. We deal with thousands of souls where our forefathers dealt with hundreds or even scores, and a much higher standard of efficiency is demanded of us than was then expected. If we are to get through our work at all, and if we are to reach more than a limited number of parishioners, our work must be done in a systematic manner.

On many points of detail I have already touched in preceding lectures. I now proceed to refer to several which have to do directly with the subject of method in our work.

The keeping of a parish book is advisable. This is distinct from the visiting directory and record of the parish which I advised last week. In fact a parish book may be subdivided into two volumes. The former will contain information on all kinds of parochial topics. The latter will describe the carrying out of various parochial work from time to time. Each volume should begin with a table of contents, and as a new subject is added to the volume it should be entered with its page in the contents. This will save much time in subsequent reference to the volume. The following are samples of entries—dimensions of church and churchyard; inventory of church plate and registers; particulars of parish work of days gone by, gleaned from time to time; parochial charities; almshouses; particulars of hospitals and convalescent homes; addresses of families in the country who will take children from the parish; church accommodation; list of laymen who will give addresses; names and addresses of members of the choir, of Sunday school teachers, and of district visitors, with their districts; people in the parish who let lodgings; duties of parochial caretakers; women who want charing or needlework; names and addresses of donors to church work, and of persons to whom the parish magazine is to be sent; list of invalids in the parish, and so forth. In volume two may be entered the following:—recipients of hospital letters; organization of Sunday schooltreats; confirmations; harvest thanksgiving services; parochial teas; missionary meetings and lectures; church decorations; sales of work; adults and children unbaptized; almanacks; recipients of relief or of invitations to old folks' dinners and the like.

Some of these will be more necessary for a Vicar than for an Assistant Curate, but every clergyman will find memoranda to add as time passes. When any annual parochial event takes place, note names of the workers, number of tickets issued and used, quantities of goods consumed, and any point in which the organization was good or defective as the case may be. Dean Butler when at Wantage used to keep 'White Books,' so called from their binding of parchment. These he described as containing "facts concerning the spiritual and bodily welfare of the parishioners of Wantage, observations on the cottages, wages, rents, marks of progression, marks of retrogression, and the like." (*Life and Letters of William John Butler*, ch. iv., p. 106.)

Few parishes can now dispense with a parish magazine. Its existence is a testimony to the power of the press. And in a parish of much organization in which large sums of money are raised and spent, a monthly magazine is absolutely indispensable. A parish magazine need not be a financial loss in a parish of fair size. Of course care must be taken in obtaining advertisements and in securing payment for them. A systematic canvas of the whole parish should be made every January. In that way subscribers who have dropped off may be recovered and new subscriptions may be obtained. The circulation will inevitably decline somewhat as the year goes on, but by the annual canvas there will be a steady growth year by year. With careful management there will be a profit on the magazine which will help some parochial fund. But if large profits are desired there must be a limit to the number of pages printed month by month. Too rigid economy may defeat its own ends. If the cover is crammed with parochial information its unattractive appearance may lose more support than is represented by the money saved in printing;

while if the events of parochial life are inadequately treated there will be a decline of interest and with it a decrease of circulation. A circulation of 1500 ought to yield a profit of ten pounds a year, while allowing ample space for parochial information. The parish magazine may thus be made to pay its way. And the business part of the work should be undertaken by laymen. The time required for successful management is not small and may take a clergyman from duties which more strictly pertain to his office. Yet trouble taken will be well repaid. Note in a book as they occur the incidents and events which should be mentioned in the next issue.

The parish magazine must be kept from the reproach brought against it by *Truth* some years ago, when its character was curtly described by that veracious journal in the words, "the twaddle of the parish magazine." We need a masculine tone in our parish magazine. The character of the work going on in the parish is reflected in its pages, and if little things loom large in the vision of the clergyman they will take up much space in the magazine, and merit the contempt of parishioners, who will gauge the clergyman through his writing if they do not know him through his preaching.

Care must also be taken to prevent the magazine from becoming a 'one man job.' Press as many pens as possible into service. Have a large reporting staff, and allow some scope for individuality and originality. At the same time if others write for the magazine, be careful to carefully look through their composition before submitting it to the printer. Mistakes of grammar will thus be avoided, as well as errors which arise from inexactness of expression.

One of my colleagues once wrote as follows : ' There is just one other service with which I think we ought to feel dissatisfied—namely, the Holy Communion." I happily detected the *lapsus calami* before the magazine was printed. What my friend was really dissatisfied with was the attendance at Holy Communion falling below its high average at his mission church.

A want of the sense of humour will sometimes make a paragraph exceptionally humorous. A lady took a party of girls to Southend for the day. In her account of their proceedings occurred a description of their trip on the water on quite a calm day. " Some of us were afraid when we saw the waves and the billows, and we were thankful to the Lord when He brought us safe to shore as He did the

s

disciples who were in the ship in the storm.
The excision of this affecting reference elicite
the rebuke from the writer that I had cu
out the spiritual part of her article, but, how
ever admirable the appreciation of the lesson
of our Lord's miracle, it was better for m
to incur the charge of unspirituality than t
cast such gems before the cynical and th
profane.

From the parish magazine to the year-boo
is quite a natural transition. The year-boo
or parochial report fills a rather different plac
from that occupied by the parish magazine. I
is specially concerned with the finances c
the parish, and will contain the balance-sheet
and statement of accounts of the various fund
connected with the church. A letter from th
Vicar reviewing the progress of the parochia
work may be included with advantage. I
attractively got up, with a few illustrations c
the parish, it will probably be read by it
recipients. In any case, it should be sen
to all subscribers and donors to parochia
funds, and to all others whose interest i
the parish it is desirable to retain or t
enlist.

The direction of these matters will li
mainly in the hands of your Vicar. At th

...me time it is well for you to see their
...earing upon the directly spiritual work in
...hich you will both be engaged. You can
...elp him much by being prompt and
...ethodical in the acknowledgment of all
...onies sent to you for the parochial funds
...r for disbursement by you in the parish.
...nd do not forget to send a stamped receipt
...romptly for the payment of your own stipend.
...e particular to note systematically every-
...ing which you are asked to do by the
...icar, and to look regularly at your memo-
...nda to see whether you have carried out
...l. Care in these matters is of the greatest
...nportance. The Vicar's burdens will pro-
...ably be heavy, and if he feels that he must
...e constantly keeping an eye on you to see
...at what he asks of you is done and to
...nsure an answer to his communications or a
...ceipt for his payments, the strain upon him
...ill be considerably increased by your want
...f thought. A little consideration will make
...ou a help to him in these matters rather
...an a hindrance. The same thing holds good
...n reference to the parish magazine. The
...icar will ask you to send in some account of
...our parochial doings before a certain date.
...ou may question whether it is desirable

for you to send in any contribution at a
But in addition to possessing other attainmen
the clergyman of to-day is expected to l
a born journalist, and one of the first requir
ments of a journalist is to know what will l
read and to make bricks without straw. Yc
will therefore rise to the occasion, and you
articles will be the very cream of the Magazin
This being interpreted is, Throw yourself int
what you write and take trouble over it. Yo
will see the importance of sending in you
articles punctually. Delay means that yo
have put off writing till the last minute, an
that consequently your article will not be s
good as it might have been. It also mean
that you are giving unnecessary trouble t
your Vicar, who is anxious to complete th
'copy' for the printer. And even if afte
sending it in punctually, you see it lyin
the next day on the Vicar's table, do not sa
to yourself, "Well, the fellow did not war
it after all," and do not promise yourself
little illicit tether next time. It does no
follow that there was not good reason fo
the Vicar's request.

The raising of funds is an anxiety in nearl
every parish. Small parishes share this anxiet
with large. The sum of money needed ther

may be less, but the number of people who are able to help is also smaller. And the equipment required for a few people is sometimes as expensive as that needed for a much larger number. In some few parishes everything necessary is provided, but this is a somewhat doubtful advantage. The resourcefulness of the people is checked and a helpful stimulus is wanting. On the other hand the parish where much is wanted and next to nothing is forthcoming imposes a terrible strain. Clergyman after clergyman is ground down and killed off by the intolerable burden. It has been said that every new church costs the life of one clergyman. To begin with, he may have scarcely enough to keep body and soul together in his own family, then he has to beg in every corner for the needs of his parish. The laity as a whole do not seem to mind. They express sympathy when some life of self-sacrifice is abruptly closed, obviously through over-strain. But even if they do not feel the injustice of imposing on the clergy burdens which the laity ought to bear, they ought to realize that it is suicidal for the Church as a fighting force to sacrifice unnecessarily some of her best men, especially in days when good men are more and more needed. There is something to be said on the other side. But even so the laity do not take their proper place. It may be partly because they are not given their share in the councils of the Church. But that is not the whole reason. Many do not come forward because they are too busy. Over what are they busy? Very often over making money. Could they not be content to make a little less money, and take their proper share in the Church's work? Some noble exceptions to the general rule prove that the busiest men sometimes find time for God's work. And a little self-sacrifice would help to combat the idea of the world that making money is the chief object in life.

In any case your Vicar will have much to do in the raising of funds. Help him in any way you can. Interest your own friends in the work of the parish. Give your own share, teach your section of parishioners to give, and collect what you can outside. Be chary of using unhallowed means for raising money. If you have bazaars, do not allow such entertainments or methods as are inconsistent with the dignity of religion or the glory of God. Forbid raffles at all costs. Do not reduce the prices of goods offered for sale below their market value. You have to raise money, but money may be bought too dearly. And in raising money you must be careful not to damage what is more precious than money—the souls of your people. In any case your bazaar will affect the local tradesmen. Large reduction in price will undersell them and be obviously prejudicial to them. It is also unfair to the donor of the article who may have laid out in money and labour more than you are asking the public to pay. Do not encourage people to squander money. The Church should teach people to be watchful over their expenditure. But to teach them economy from the pulpit is useless and inconsistent, if you teach them extravagance in your bazaar. Do not bother people into helping. The words 'God loveth a cheerful giver' are just as true of gifts in kind or in labour, as of gifts in coin. And do not be unfair to tradesmen, by first damaging their trade and then asking them to subscribe, to give goods, to pay for advertisements in your programme, and also to come to purchase what they do not require. You may if not careful make the Church fairly stink in their nostrils. But tact, thought, and prayer will here, as elsewhere, enable you to steer the right course.

Do not preach 'begging' sermons often. By all means preach on the duty of almsgiving and of being systematic in giving, and of setting aside a proportion of income for God. But nothing is more damaging than to be continually hammering at people because they give only a penny each on the average. Lay down the right principle. See that the people are actuated by the right motive to follow that principle—namely, the constraining love of Christ. And when some excellent object for their gifts is brought before them, explain the interest and the worthiness of the object in a few terse and telling sentences, mentioning what will strike their imagination, and leave the rest to their conscience and to God. Money squeezed out of people ceases to be an offering. And in God's sight a small sum may be of more value than a large.

In issuing printed appeals for money, every-thing depends on the way the work is done. The utmost care must be expended over the framing of the appeal, the shape and the size, the words and the pictures. Even the handwriting on the envelope is of importance. Appeals scattered wholesale may cost more money than they produce. They should be sent to names carefully chosen, and a short letter from the sender should accompany them. A long letter will probably be put into the waste-paper basket unread. Let your letter be legible, neat and concise. A short letter may take you a longer time to write than a long one. But in any case take trouble over it. It may bring you a donation of five pounds. And if it fails through any fault of your own, your negligence will be costly.

Some clergymen raise large sums by personally interviewing likely donors. This is doubtless a most efficacious way of raising funds, but it is not everyone who can adopt it. I never have the pluck or the cheek, whichever it is, to adopt this course, and I always fancy that I have not the time. But if you are gifted with a winning personality, especially with a magnetism which attracts gold and cheques, by all means exercise the gifts with which you are blessed.

Be very careful to keep a strict account of all monies passing through your hands. It is well to pass everything through the bank. But in any case note every item in your ledger, and at the end of the financial year make up your accounts and have a balance sheet ready for your Vicar's inspection or for printing in the year-book. "Provide things honest in the sight of all men" (Romans xii. 17).

Exercise caution also in your disbursements. Cleverness at raising funds will not justify you in extravagance. Waste of God's money cannot be too severely condemned, especially when it is so much needed in many quarters. Do not embark on unnecessary schemes. Too ambitious a project initiated by a capable Vicar in one parish may prevent a less skilful, but equally needy brother in another parish from obtaining what he asks for very modest requirements. It may also seriously cripple his successor.

In raising and disbursing funds always remember that money alone cannot ensure the blessing of God. Vast sums may be raised, yet the blessing of God may be withheld. And even where money is short, blessing may be richly given. It is not always well for a church to be rich and increased with goods. And though money may represent the offerings of God's people for work in a particular place, and though, if people withhold their offerings, the work cannot be done, yet there is a danger of allowing the raising of money to be the most prominent factor in parochial organization and to become more important than the winning of souls.

Associated with these subjects is the difficult work of relief of the sick and needy. This is not an exact science. Theorists give us plenty of advice, but they do not always agree, and practical men contradict one another. In the same series of books on practical work one writer advises the clergyman to give food and coals to the poor only by tickets or orders on local tradesmen, another considers the system of tickets most pernicious and advocates giving help in money. The work of charitable relief calls for several qualities and for not a little knowledge. Some acquaintance with economics and social science will be useful, and a study of Charity Organization Society principles will also help. One may or may not agree with the methods of the Charity Organization Society, but undoubted wisdom and experience lie at the base of their work. *The Charities Register and Digest* contains most valuable articles on the subject, and you will probably be able to borrow a copy from your Vicar. It ought to be in his study, if it is not. But it is so needful an adjunct to charitable work that you must not keep a borrowed copy for long. A second-hand copy should be obtainable for one or two shillings. Lay down some rules for yourself before you begin work, and modify these rules as experience may demand. Never lend money. It is better to give a little than to lend much. Never give to anyone whom you do not know. Do not grudge the time or trouble to go to his house, if you are unacquainted with the person who asks for relief.

Ascertain from your Vicar how much alms money you are to be allowed for your district each month, and see that the amount is not exceeded. If it be insufficient, try to collect a few subscriptions for your special needs. Do not give relief to children who come on behalf of their parents, unless you are sure that it is impossible for either to come in person. Every one admits in theory at least that doles are most objectionable, and yet every one continues to give them. But it is best to aim at helping fewer cases and giving those more liberal help. The gift of doles is certainly apt to foster a spirit of dependence, and to encourage people to muddle along anyhow. But they may be the means of keeping off starvation, and perhaps a dole now and again might have saved the life of the poor fellow of thirty-seven who died of starvation at Hackney the other day, and whom his wife watched grow weaker from day to day without being able to relieve their want. The scanty and precarious earnings of many London families make the practice of thrift almost impossible. The effects of sickness in the home or of a bout of lack of employment are scarcely got over before the husband is out of work and debt begins again to accumulate. At the same time the week of our working people is apt to be somewhat self-contained. What is received during a good week is often spent at once, so that a bad week is struggled through without anything to fall back on.

Sick clubs and thrift clubs are desirable adjuncts to parish work, and if there be nothing of the kind in your district except in connection with the public-houses, you might organize some for men and for women. The principle of slate clubs, on which the balance in hand is divided amongst the members at the end of the year, is generally considered unsound. Thrift thus exercised does not lead to any permanent result. Each year stands and falls by itself. And nothing is done to provide for old age. If possible, do not form an independent society. Found a branch of the National Deposit Friendly Society, or of some other society, which has a sound constitution and good rules, and whose basis will assure your own club more than a precarious existence. In any event be careful in your dealings with the money of parishioners. See that it is in safe hands, and that the system of checking receipts and payments is business-like and thorough.

From time to time there will be special services or meetings which will require careful organization. This may be just the work in which you can relieve your Vicar of much unnecessary labour. He will probably assign you certain duties in connection with these various events. If he does not, and especially if he be not in your humble opinion—as is very likely—a good organizer, ask him to write down a list of particular duties for which he wishes you to be responsible.

Carry out your duties with thoroughness, but without fuss or noise. Picture in your own mind what will take place, and think what arrangements will be necessary and what books or articles must be in particular places. Then have a mental rehearsal and see that everything is right. Careful thought in preparation is essential to the smooth working of many parochial functions. And organization may be in this connection a friend and a neighbour of spirituality. A Confirmation may be held at your church, and if the arrangements have not been carefully thought out, one or two hitches may rob the Service of reverence and solemnity, and may take the minds of some of the candidates off the blessing of God which they have come to seek. In connection with many parochial engagements, such as missionary meetings, you may find special methods necessary to ensure a large attendance. The printing must be judicious. There must be no stinting, but effective printing is more important than wholesale. Draw up your bills carefully beforehand, and shew the printer exactly how you wish the type to be arranged. Adequate notice in church is useful, and a word or two which will appeal to the imagination will be far better than the mere hackneyed announcement that a meeting of a particular society will be held at such a time and place, and that Mr. Jones, from Africa, will be the deputation. On certain occasions send to each communicant a printed notice of the meeting or service; a portrait with a few particulars of the work of the expected speaker will often increase the attendance at and the interest in the meeting. In this work you can enlist the aid of some of your people. Organize a band of workers who will see that notices are left at every house in the parish, each undertaking a particular street, and requisition them when anything special is in view. It is scarcely fair to ask a deputation to address a small meeting or preach to a handful of people, and there is the further consideration that a great opportunity is lost if you do not make use of his visit to further the cause in hand. Unfortunately some clergymen view the visit of a deputation as an occasion for going away for a Sunday, or at any rate for having an easy time, and the deputation is discouraged, the opportunity becomes a mere routine engagement, and coldness takes possession of audience or congregation.

Enter in the second volume of your parish books particulars of the service or meeting, mentioning any faults, and read up your entries before making your arrangements in a succeeding year.

Besides noting all your engagements as you make them in a pocket diary (see page 160), note in a list the names of persons whom you are asked to visit or of whose special circumstances you may hear. Carry out faithfully all that you undertake. Do not draw back from any engagement without urgent cause. And do not alter your arrangements on any but most certain evidence. Four old public school boys were serving with a military expedition in South Africa. One day they went to see some sporting contest in the neighbourhood, intending to return to camp in time for the inspection ordered by their colonel. But a man arrived with the news that the inspection had been cancelled. As he stayed, they did the same, only to find on their return to camp that their authority was misinformed. For their breach of discipline they were placed under arrest, court-martialled, and sent home for some months' seclusion in Brixton Military Prison. You will not want to go to races nor will you be sent to gaol, but a similar mistake on your part may cause a wedding or burial party to be kept waiting for an hour or two, and to suffer serious inconvenience. And the way such an error is regarded in the army on service should lead us to take

T

a serious view of such failings in work fc
God.

The need of care, method and exactnes
comes up at all points, and you will alway
be repaid in adopting the motto of the Ea
of Strafford, "Thorough." A common tend
ency to-day is to cover much ground in
slipshod way; to attempt too many thing
imperfectly; and to forget that engagement
are opportunities for promoting the Kingdor
of God—the great purpose of your Ordina
tion.

What I have said may seem to point to th
elaboration of statistics. There is no doul
that statistics are useful. Some clergyme
talk glibly about leaving results to God, whe
no results of their work are apparent, or c
not believing in statistics when there are non
worth recording, or when they are too laz
to record them. But while as careful t
tabulate your work and its results as t
think out your methods, do not worshi
statistics. They are rather for your ow
guidance than for announcement to th
world. And excessive publication of statistic
leads to a desire to 'break the record' fror
year to year. Everything must be force
up to a high level, and after a few years th

maximum is reached. When figures begin to shew a decline, the incumbent feels that his work in the parish is done, and he hears a call to go elsewhere—not necessarily to the foreign mission-field, but to some other corner of the vineyard at home.

And when the records are broken there is the tendency to publish the news to the ecclesiastical world, which is too ready to substitute for more solid reading the devouring of ecclesiastical gossip. It may be said that a certain amount of advertisement is necessary to draw to one's coffers the gifts of the faithful, and that if the details of one's work are not familiar financial support will not be forthcoming. But one needs to be specially modest about one's achievements, when one considers how poor one's best is and how slow the best men of the world are to publish their deeds in their own line of life. I will not say anything of less honourable motives than the advertisement of parochial needs. There may or may not be men who indulge, or get others to indulge, in pious puffing of their work. But Bishop Fraser seemed to think in his time that there were men who indulged in 'self-advertisement' from the most sordid motives, for he wrote in 1862 :

"Nothing is more sickening than the attempt of the so-called working clergy to obtrude their work and their merits on the notice of the world" (*Life*, page 112).

So far as possible, train others to share your work. Remember always that here is an important part of your ministry. Be on the lookout for work for all to do, and for workers to carry out the work. Try to get so much of your work as possible done by others. There will still be plenty left which only you can do. Set every communicant to some work. And though you will always inspire and encourage your fellow-workers, do not let them expect you to be ever at their side or at their back. Train them to be so far self-reliant that they shall not lean continually on you to help them; yet not to be self-reliant in another sense, in that they must ever lean on God for grace and power. Teach them how to do their work, and give them hints from time to time. Train young men to speak in public, bring them on to take that share of ministration which God may be now shewing—by the growth of population, the opening of new doors and the decrease of candidates for Holy Orders. —that He would have laymen to undertake.

In every department of your work be systematic and methodical. And remember the connection of careful organization with spiritual power. " He that is faithful in a very little is faithful also in much " (St. Luke xvi. 10). Dr. Latham in his *Pastor Pastorum* understands the 'little' as answering to "the externals of religious management," and the 'much' to 'the spiritual verity which passes from soul to soul "—in other words, he that is faithful in parochial organization will also be faithful in exerting truly spiritual influence, and in imparting spiritual truth. Dr. Latham writes (page 397, eleventh thousand), "those who are unfaithful in matters of administration which are comparatively little, will find that this spreading laxity will overthrow their whole nature and that they will soon be unfaithful in that which is great."

X.

FINALITY.

"I AM A and Ω, the Beginning and the End."
Our lectures began with Christ; with Him
they must end. The Good Shepherd must
be the Pattern and Example for all His
servants. At the same time it will be well
for us to 'mark the perfect men and to behold
the upright,' in order that we may follow them
even as they followed Christ. From them we
may learn how to take the yoke of Christ
and how to bear His burden, how to feed and
to tend His flock.

In our daily life we shall therefore observe
the methods of living masters of spiritual
Israel, but at first at any rate we shall have
a better opportunity of becoming acquainted
with the best men and their methods in the
biographies of notable parish priests.

Enlarge continually your circle of such

acquaintances. Draw not from one century, but from several; not from the home mission-field only, but from the foreign as well. Do not confine your choice to men of your own school of thought or even of your own Church. There are many men and many minds amongst the clergy of to-day. And however gravely you may differ from some, it is your duty to try to understand them, and this the biographies of men of varying views will help you to do. And you must be willing to learn from any one, even if in your estimation he be an 'enemy.'

I propose to briefly review the work of several parish priests of various ages in the later history of the Church of England.

Readers of Bishop Lightfoot's *Leaders of the Northern Church* can hardly help loving Bernard Gilpin, Rector of Houghton-le-Spring, Durham. The Bishop tells us that "Bernard Gilpin was the true product of the English Reformation, born with its birth, growing with its growth, yielding up his spirit to God at the moment of its consummation. He was its noblest representative also. He appropriated only its excellencies, while he was altogether free from its faults. He lost nothing that was valuable in the old, and he apprehended all that was true in the new." But it is not on this account merely that I commend to you the study of his character. For—as the Bishop tells us—"he was the prototype of the English parish clergyman. Even at this late date, after the lapse of three centuries, he is still the best model on which the priest can frame and fashion his life. He anticipated too by three centuries the supplemental work, which in our own age for the first time the clergy have grafted upon their parochial ministrations" (pp. 131, 132).

A window in Durham Cathedral commemorates Bernard Gilpin. And as I cannot summarize here his remarkable career, the window may tell us its own story. The first light represents Gilpin as giving away his horse. When he was out riding in his parish one day, he came across a little group of parishioners. One was in great trouble, as a horse in the team with which he was ploughing had fallen dead. Gilpin dismounted, and offered him his own horse. The parishioner replied that it would be a long time before he could pay for such a horse as that, whereupon Gilpin took off the bridle and saddle, ordered the man to send them to the Rectory and told him to take the horse, announcing that he would send for the money when he wanted it. The incident is characteristic of Gilpin's open-handed generosity to his parishioners. Never did a man live up more faithfully to the principles of the Sermon on the Mount. Every Thursday he cooked a large quantity of meat for the poor, while every day he provided broth for the needy, thus instituting a sixteenth century soup-kitchen. Twenty-four of the poorest parishioners he regarded as his own pensioners. Yet there was a hint of modern methods in the care with which he inquired into the circumstances of the needy—aiming specially at finding out those whose modesty would prevent them from asking aid. He liked best to lay out money which would encourage industry.

The second light in the window represents Gilpin as quelling a 'deadly feud' in Rothbury Church. Armed members of two hostile clans fell out during the service. Gilpin descended from the pulpit and with great courage separated the ringleaders. He induced them to keep the peace so long as he was in the church, and then preached a sermon on the wickedness of settling a feud by resort to arms. The incident illustrates Gilpin's courage. He cared not for his foes, who

were numerous, nor did he fear the wrath of
Queen Mary. And when Bishop Bonner sent
to arrest him with the intention of bringing
him to the stake within a fortnight, he expressed himself willing to die and ordered a
long white garment in which to be burnt.
The death of the Queen set him free to continue his courageous ministry. The scandals
of pluralism and non-residence, the misdeeds
of ecclesiastical authorities, and the vices of
the times were bravely exposed.

The third light in the Durham window
illustrates Gilpin founding Houghton Grammar
School. Gilpin's care for the children and zeal
for education were unfailing. Not only did he
found the School, and give financial assistance
to numerous scholars, but every year he
assisted some eight or nine of the boys to
proceed to the universities. One who was
thus helped subsequently became Bishop of
Chichester.

One or two other characteristics of Gilpin
mark him out as worthy of our attention.

He was disinterested and conscientious to
a degree. More than once he resigned
ecclesiastical appointments when he felt that
he could not do justice to the demands of
the positions. On one such occasion his

uncle, Bishop Tunstall, of Durham, offered
him a dispensation to retain a benefice without fulfilling the duties of the charge. This
he scorned to accept. The bishopric of
Carlisle was offered to him, but he refused it
in spite of pressure on the ground that he
must either remain dumb or speak out against
many with whom he was connected by ties
of relationship or of acquaintance.

Perhaps above all Gilpin's character should
appeal to us for his absolute sincerity and
love of truth. He lived in times of great
uncertainty and division. He ministered in
the reigns of Henry VIII., Edward VI., Mary
and Elizabeth. Gilpin did not throw in his
lot with one side, and then, blinded by strong
prejudices, hold fast in pride and obstinacy
to the position which he had adopted. He
was open-minded enough to receive new light
upon any subject, and his desire was at all
costs to find truth. So he reviewed and revised his position as time went on. Yet
Gilpin was no Vicar of Bray. Throughout
he was honest and straightforward, and when
he reached his convictions nothing would move
him from them or restrain their expression.
In his younger days Gilpin had held a public
disputation with Bishop Hooper. Later on,

when Peter Martyr was challenged to a public discussion at Oxford, Gilpin was one of four chosen to oppose him. His singular fairness and obvious sincerity attracted Peter Martyr's respect, so much so that the Regius Professor said that Gilpin's advocacy was a credit to his cause. These disputations led Gilpin to see the weakness of his own position, and he made further inquiry, not resting until after thought and study both at home and abroad he satisfied himself as to the position of the Church of Rome and as to that of the English Reformers. The history of his spiritual experience is full of teaching for the young clergyman who may be tempted to ally himself with a particular side in Church matters and blindly accept its conclusions rather than to sift things for himself. It should be equally useful to one who may be in a state of mental and spiritual uncertainty, and who while called to teach others, feels that on some points he scarcely knows where he stands himself.

Passing from the north-east of England to the south-west and from the sixteenth century to the eighteenth, we find a parish priest of rare spiritual power in Samuel Walker, Curate of Truro. We are sometimes tempted to think that certain methods of work are the discovery of our own time. Sidney's biography removes misconception on this score, and Walker's methods do not seem at all antiquated in the present day. Samuel Walker was born at Exeter in A.D. 1714. He was educated at Exeter Grammar School and at Exeter College, Oxford, and at the age of 23 years he was ordained to a country Curacy in Devonshire. He wrote afterwards that the week before his ordination he "spent with the other candidates . . . dining, supping, drinking and laughing together, when God knows we should have been all on our knees, and warning each other to fear for our souls in the view of what we were about to put our hands to." Walker's second Curacy was at Lanlivery, in Cornwall, with the Archdeacon of Totnes, on whose death soon afterwards Walker was appointed Vicar 'in commendam,' until a nephew of the patron was eligible to hold the family living. Walker's work at Lanlivery was significant, because to all appearances in a decadent age it was that of an earnest parish priest. We are told that he was an attractive preacher, and that "his decorous life and fascinating manners ensured him much affection and respect. He reproved, exhorted, and watched over the people of his flock, preaching, catechising, and visiting diligently in private." When a dangerous illness overtook him, he dictated a letter to be sent to certain parishioners named by him, who had refused to listen to his warnings. But the six years' ministry at Lanlivery he afterwards felt to have been defective at foundation. On resigning the benefice Walker accepted a Curacy at St. Mary's, Truro, now merged in the Cathedral. He went there for the sake of the society and amusements which were to be found there. And for a year he shone in social life as also in the pulpit. But his acquaintance with Mr. Conon, Master of the Truro Grammar School, was destined to put a new complexion on his ministry. Under the influence of Mr. Conon he was led to see that he had been actuated by a desire of reputation and a love of pleasure, and that he knew little of the power of our Lord to save him personally from sin.

The character of Walker's ministry was now transformed. The record of his work shows how much may be accomplished by an Assistant Curate, whose whole life is consecrated to God and directed by the Holy Spirit. Many of Walker's former friends turned against him when he preached in plain terms on the nature of sin, the judgment of God and salvation through Christ. But his example and preaching won him friends in other quarters, and his popularity for social gifts—a snare to many a clergyman to-day—gave place to affection for his spiritual qualities. Crowds flocked to St. Mary's Church to hear him preach. It was popularly said that during the hours of divine service cannon might be fired down the main street without hitting anyone. What was more important still, numbers of people resorted to Walker for spiritual counsel and direction, and he states that in the course of a few years some 800 people came to him privately in anxiety about their spiritual condition. These figures are remarkable in a country town so small as Truro was at that time. And the moral effects resembled somewhat those of which we read just now in South Wales. The theatre and the cock-pit were closed, and drunkenness and immorality diminished.

Walker's methods of work are of great interest. He drew up a scheme for the private instruction of those who resorted to him, and carefully grounded his converts in the doctrines of the Christian faith. He organized what we might call prayer circles, each of which consisted of some six or seven persons, and which met weekly for intercessory prayer. He also formed two 'societies,' one for unmarried men, the other for married men, their wives, and unmarried women.

It might be supposed that there was some departure from Church order in the work which Walker carried out. So far from this being the case he was particular to a degree in the regulations which he imposed. Communicants only were eligible for membership. Walker was very chary of allowing any member of his societies to offer prayer or to give an address in his own presence. His influence was paramount throughout.

In Walker were blended the most intense spiritual fervour and the strictest regard for Church order, and one may see in his methods means by which the fruits of genuine revival may be retained and made permanent within the Church. If God be pleased to send a gracious reviving again upon our land, why should not the stream of blessing flow right through our churches instead of having to force some irregular channel which may avoid them in its course? But we must be ready, and there must be in us no obstruction to the flow of blessing, which might cause its flood to seek a different channel.

Walker was a keen advocate of catechizing. He deplored its neglect in his own days, and wanted to bring the matter before the Archbishop of Canterbury. He had three Catechisms in St. Mary's Church—one for children under twelve years of age, a second for young people between the ages of twelve and fifteen years, and a third for young people over fifteen and under twenty years of age. His catechizing was systematic—suggestive of the methods of to-day, and conducted in the presence of a large congregation, which often numbered five hundred adults.

Another feature of Walker's ministry was the value which he set upon the Prayer Book. He preached courses of sermons on various parts of it, in order to train his people to take an intelligent share in its offices, and he drew up a treatise on *The Daily Service*, which he lent for private reading amongst those whom he instructed.

Persevering for years in faithful work in one parish, Walker rose in the estimation of those who desired the progress of true religion. It was not to be wondered at that he became the friend and adviser of John Wesley. But he found himself continually in conflict with the teaching of Wesley himself and with the practices of his adherents. Wesley he charged with including assurance within the definition of saving faith and therefore of making sad many whom God had not made sad. Wesley's disciples and lay-preachers he charged with irregularity in their methods of itinerant preaching, and with laxity in their conformity to Church discipline and indeed in their adhesion to the Church itself.

At the same time Walker was disliked by many of his clerical neighbours. He was regarded and treated at Truro much as Henry Martyn was some fifty years later. But a Walker window and a Henry Martyn baptistry and anniversary sermon in Truro Cathedral shew that the ecclesiastical authorities of to-day possess a wider appreciation of their merits than did those of their own times. Yet Walker's worth was discerned by some, and several offers of preferment were pressed upon him. These he stedfastly declined, deciding to remain in a subordinate position amongst his loved people at Truro. So he lived on and worked there for fourteen years, till enfeebled by consumption he had to seek change and rest. Amongst his admirers was the Earl of Dartmouth, and it was during a visit to the Earl at Blackheath Hill that his gentle spirit returned to God who gave it in July, 1761, at the age of 46. His remains were buried in the churchyard of Lewisham, where the parish registers give a simple record of the burial.

Coming down to the last generation we can study with profit such a biography as that of Bishop Thorold. Mr. Simpkinson does not tell us much about his early life, but we learn that at Oxford he did not work hard, to his great regret in after life (*Bishop Thorold*, Simpkinson, ch. i.). From the earlier part of Bishop Thorold's career we learn how genuine spirituality may be blended with thoroughness in parochial work and organization. A London daily paper honoured the Biography with a leading article instead of a review when the book was published, but it spoke sneeringly of a young clergyman of twenty-five writing to a parishioner who was thought to be dying in the following terms: "We do not think enough how gracious and condescending in God it is to *take the trouble* to afflict us" (p. 21). But the long letter quoted breathes an air of beautiful spirituality and must have been very comforting to its recipient, who was alive nearly fifty years

afterwards at the age of 95 when the book
was written. In Thorold's first Curacy—at
Whittington, a country parish—he records 119
lectures on the Bible and 1431 pastoral visits
in one year. By all means read the quotations
from his visiting journal. They enable us to
see one of the very best of parochial visitors
at work.

After five years Thorold moved to Holy
Trinity, Marylebone. Here he had a district
of 3000 people. In the first year he visited
the district "twice through, going into every
room of every house." He spent 15 hours
weekly in visiting, and his visits averaged over
50 weekly or 2700 each year. As Rector of
St. Giles' (1857 to 1868) Thorold did a remarkable work, not the least feature of which was
his erection of new schools at a cost of
£16,000. From 1869 to 1877 Thorold was
Vicar of St. Pancras.

The record of his life at St. Giles' and St.
Pancras reminds us that the busiest of town
clergy can find time for adequate preparation
of sermons, and that a high spiritual tone
can be maintained amid constant pressure of
work. "Intellectually," we are told, "he was
interesting; spiritually he had begun to exercise
that irresistible fascination by which the true

lover of God draws other souls heavenwards"
(p. 39). His preaching was "imaginative,
dramatic, incisive, and devout" (p. 58). "The
principal object which he proposed to himself
was the personal conversion to God of each
worshipper" (p. 58). Later on Thorold was
called to higher service in the sees of Rochester
and of Winchester successively till his death
in 1895.

The records of Church work contain the
story of many men of worth and power whose
work is none the less noteworthy because their
names are not familiar to every Churchman.
The Rev. Canon Hobson resigned the charge
of St. Nathaniel's, Liverpool, in 1901, after
an incumbency of 33 years. He published in
1903 an autobiography,[1] in a preface to which
the Bishop of Liverpool says: "Canon Hobson's story is a proof that the poorest in the
land may be led to love our national Church,
and to support it and to work for it with a self-
denial and enthusiasm which put to shame
many of our educated people" (p. xiv). In
another quarter Canon Hobson's work has
met with commendation, as Sir Baldwyn
Leighton, a worshipper of St. Alban's, Hol-
born, gave a most favourable account of the

[1] *What hath God Wrought?* (Elliot Stock, 1903).

parish at the Manchester Church Congress in 1888 (p. 325).

The book is noteworthy as shewing how Canon Hobson began his clerical career at the age of 34 years with few advantages, and how after three years' work in Birkenhead he was planted down in ' 16 acres of sin' to begin a work for God which has been marvellously blessed. I have no personal knowledge of Canon Hobson, but I never shall forget seeing his church crowded with the very poorest folk at the opening of a mission in January, 1890, when the late Bishop Ryle preached the sermon and the present Bishop of Winchester took part in the service.

In bidding public farewell to the Vicar, Bishop Chavasse said that the secret of Canon Hobson's success and powerful ministry was his careful parochial work. Into some of the details of that work it may be useful to look. The Vicar began in a cellar, and on the first evening one man, three women and a small boy formed the congregation. But from the first the work grew rapidly, and within a few months forty candidates were presented for Confirmation. The church was built to hold 700 people, and was consecrated after eight months' work; but the congregations were so large that after two years the seating accommodation was increased to provide for over 1000 worshippers. Still the people poured in, and the work progressed, and by 1882 there was a roll of 800 communicants, a large proportion of whom were parishioners.

What were the main principles of the work? First and foremost incessant pastoral visitation. Nearly twenty times is the importance of this duty emphasized in the book. To it in the earlier years of his incumbency Canon Hobson gave six hours a day for five days in the week, and three hours on Saturdays. His visits were of a teaching character, using any opportunity for dropping a few appropriate words as a seed. "The lion's share of time and strength" was "given to the Godless, the indifferent and the nominal professors" (p. 151). Not that the Vicar had a natural gift for this work. At the outset of his ministry he shrank from pastoral visitation as a "task too formidable . . . to achieve" (p. 43). He therefore cast himself on the Lord, claiming the needed grace, and on the strength of his commission he went forward, finding that the stone of difficulty was rolled away. But even in after years perseverance

was still needed, and here the experience of
Canon Hobson as an incessant visitor corro-
borates that of Canon Savage, for he says:
"Such work taxes the energies, tries the
patience, and tests the love of the visitor.
It will be given up, with many apparently
justifying reasons, unless there be a daily
supply of Divine grace" (pp. 83, 84). Canon
Hobson strongly urges the refusal of outside
work, as tending to interfere with the most
important of parochial duties.

Another feature of his work was the care of
the children. The Vicar laid himself out to
win their love, and even the ragged schools
returned his devotion with the most genuine
affection. The children of the parish smashed
76 panes of glass in the church in the nine
days which elapsed between the glazing of the
windows and the consecration, but the love of
the children for the Vicar made his instruction
to them on the subject of the church as God's
House efficacious, and for 30 years no wiring
was needed to protect the windows. Much
care was taken with the Sunday Schools, and
they always held the upper hand in the parish,
though no prizes were ever given. Few of the
children of the parish remained outside Sunday
School influence.

This led up to Confirmation work, which was a special feature at St. Nathaniel's, the service nearly always taking place on Whitsunday. The second year's Confirmation saw 141 candidates for Confirmation, out of whom 106 were confirmed. In 1877 out of 131 candidates in the classes 103 were confirmed. In 1899 ninety were confirmed. Special pains were taken over the preparation, and conversion was pressed as a necessary condition of presentation to the Bishop. A large proportion of those who were confirmed and who remained in the neighbourhood continued communicants. The means used for retaining them were threefold—(1) enrolling them in some Bible-class; (2) giving them some work to do for the church or parish; (3) carefully and lovingly shepherding them. The people were thoroughly interested in their church, and were made to feel that it belonged to them; and the church was made as good in every respect as it could possible be. The services were so arranged that all could take part in them. Spiritual work was put first of all factors for the elevation of the degraded in the parish. In every department of work for God the Holy Spirit's blessing was specially sought. The "spiritual regeneration of souls,

and their sanctification " was the one great aim
in all the church work.   Only communicants
were eligible to act as church wardens, sidesmen, teachers, singers, visitors, or regular
church workers.   The staff of clergy was very
small, the Vicar at times being single-handed,
but he accomplished much by refusing to do
work which could be done by others.   The
Vicar was accessible to his people at all times.
In financial matters the church was not allowed
to get into debt.   Laymen were carefully
trained to take up work—"as much spiritual
work as" possible, "within the limits of
Church order."   And on resignation of the
charge Canon Hobson left more than fifty
men fit to lead in prayer and to give addresses.

Preaching occupied a prominent place in the
work, and the Vicar not only gave careful
preparation to his sermons, but aimed at
preparing when fresh rather than leaving this
work till he was overtired.   The organization
of parochial agencies was not forced on.   A
fresh society was only established when needed,
and therefore lived and thrived the longer.
The moral effects of the work were clearly
traceable in the parish.   The tenants of the
houses became more regular in payment of
their rents.   Ladies could traverse the worst

streets without fear of molestation. Scandalous behaviour outside the church at weddings ceased. Sickness in the parish decreased one-half. Numbers of fallen women were dealt with, and many degraded lives were changed—fully justifying the title of the autobiography, *What hath God Wrought?* and sufficing to inspire the candidate for Holy Orders with confidence as to the possibilities in work for God even in the most degraded districts.

Enough of biographies to remind us of the importance of reading carefully several every year. Do not confine your biographical reading to clerical memoirs. The occasional reading of biographies of such laymen as Sir Arthur Blackwood or the Earl of Shaftesbury, or even of Nonconformist ministers of eminence like Dr. Dale, of Birmingham, will keep you from the spirit of officialism in your work for God, and will give you many ideas which will help you to become more resourceful and effective in your work. You will be the better able to see the point of view of those from whom you differ, or of those to whom you minister, and you will be helped to shew yourselves ministers approved unto God.

The reading of clerical biographies will also

help you to guard against settling down to work in a groove. It will prevent you from being content with a low standard of work. It will forbid you to think that you cannot accomplish much. It will remind you that many men who have finished well began with fewer advantages than your own. It will shew you the growth of the characters and of the work of holy men of God. It will prevent you from becoming narrow, jealous or exclusive. It will remind you that there are diversities of gifts, but the same Spirit. Where spiritual blessing has been given, it has been through the consecration of all gifts to God's service for the Holy Spirit to use as He may direct. We are scarcely beginning to learn—still less to exhaust—the meaning of the command, "Be filled with the Spirit" (Ephesians v. 18).

Study the Bible for the daily renewal of your own spirit, and for that growth in grace without which your ministry cannot be spiritual. Correct your understanding of the principles on which you will work by study of the Bible and good commentaries, the Prayer Book and works on dogmatic theology. Correct the methods of exercising your ministry by the study of books on various branches of pastoral work and biographies of notable parish priests. Each year will then see you more skilled as a workman in the factory of God.

Whatever you believe, be true to that. A parishioner who for years had been a most active secularist worker and speaker, but who was brought to Christ through one of the Nonconformist denominations, told me that once in his atheistic days he was very ill. I asked him whether he felt uneasy at the thought of approaching death. He said " No —only so far as I had not been true to my own conscience : it was inconsistency with my belief alone that troubled me." A truth lies here. Consistency is of great value. But it is not the only thing. The sceptic was not right in his belief. And in answer to his wife's prayers offered for many years he afterwards found that it mattered very much what a man believed, and he learnt the Gospel, and now lives true to that. And I feel sure that you will bring your belief to the standard of God's Word, and that you will try at all times to be true to what you believe. "Thanks be to God," wrote St. Paul to the Romans (vi. 17, R.V.), "that, whereas ye were servants of sin, ye became obedient from the heart to that form of teaching whereunto ye were delivered."

One feature you will find to be common to all men of spiritual power—they have always been men of prayer. On this sufficient stress may not have been laid in these lectures. Before closing the subject may I urge once more the importance of prayer as a thread running through the whole texture of our work? Be systematic and definite in your private prayer. Never let public prayer take the place of or encroach upon your private devotions. You may find a little book by Dr. C. F. Harford, entitled *Daily*, useful for the entry of persons or subjects for which you wish to pray regularly. One of my own colleagues is publishing a little book for similar use by our parishioners. Use if possible the *Cycle of Prayer for Foreign Missions*, published by the Church Missionary Society, or some kindred paper of intercessions. Remember really to pray when you are engaged in the services of the Church and keep worshippers up to their duty in this respect. Expect the prayers offered in church to be answered. Teach your people to look upon Morning and Evening Prayer as the Church's Prayer Meeting, but give them the opportunity of meeting weekly for extempore prayer as well. Encourage them to pray for the sick by name in the Church services, and ask their prayers in Church for any parochial project of importance. Inculcate the observance of family prayer in Christian homes. Recommend suitable manuals for such purposes when the head of the house shrinks from using his own words. Offer prayer at the beginning or end of parochial functions, whenever possible. It may be felt by some that the sanctity of prayer is thereby impaired, but if your work is on spiritual lines, such a practice will teach the people to engage in nothing which they cannot ask God to bless, and to regard it as possible to hallow what are considered the most secular duties and works. Thus the incense of intercessory prayer will be continually ascending from your own heart, your church and your parish as a sweet-smelling savour to God.

Meantime the work of shepherding Christ's flock will be going on. The purpose of Christ's death was that He should gather together in one the children of God that were scattered abroad (St. John xi. 52). For the accomplishment of that purpose you are working. And faith in the Holy Spirit will enable you to believe that the Lord has much people in the city or village where He calls you to work. It is yours to search out Christ's sheep, having faith enough to believe that any lost one may be brought into the fold and numbered with the flock; zeal and love enough to take any trouble to win even a single soul; perseverance enough not to be content with bringing it merely to the door of the fold; and imagination enough to see that any act or word of yours may attract or repel the lost one. "Promote as much as lieth in you peace and love among all Christian people," that the prayer of our Lord may be realized, and that all may be one—one with Him and in Him.

So your work will go on—watching over the lambs in infancy and childhood, and the sheep in the various stages of the Christian course—'in all time of their tribulation; in all time of their wealth, and in the hour of death'; and laying them to rest in sure and certain hope of the Resurrection to eternal life.

The effect of our work is not only to be traced in what people think can be seen in the parish. Its influence extends to many a thought, word and deed which might have been different, if we had not been there. And though at times it may seem as if there is little to shew for our ministry, yet it is impossible to calculate how far things would have been different if our influence had been withdrawn. And some of our people will have left the parish, even if it be a country parish of small population, and will have carried our influence to perhaps remote corners of the earth. But when all is said and done, the effect of much of our work must be visible only to the eye of God.

In a large parish we shall often, perhaps once or twice weekly, part through death with a dweller in our district. Much time and thought may have been spent in ministering to them ere they start on the last journey. And of many, in some cases after a faithful life, in others after repentance at the last, we may entertain a good hope. And though in many cases the good which men do is not interred with their bones, yet we shall often feel that the best fruit of our work we are burying beneath the ground. But we need not grieve at that. Man's ways are not God's ways. And as the farmer hesitates not to bury some of the best of his grain in the hope that a rich harvest will thereby be yielded, so we may feel that our labour is not in vain in the Lord, but that when we lay to rest the body

x

of some loved parishioner, it is but the falling of the corn of wheat into the ground that —dying and abiding alone—it may bring forth much fruit.

When I pay a visit to the parish in the far west where for over six years my lot was cast, I always like to spend a few minutes in the little cemetery, where many of the faithful to whom I ministered in days gone by are laid to rest. Call it not morbid. Much of the fruit of my work is now buried in the acre of God. And so I like to pass from grave to grave, noting the familiar and much-loved names—some who finished their course with peace, some who finished it even with joy. For them one needs not to pray now, for the souls of the righteous are in the hands of God, but it is well to offer praise for those who have departed this life in His faith and fear, and to pray that with them we may enter His everlasting Kingdom.

Each year the number grows—one and another of Christ's sheep are gathered into the heavenly fold. And one's own turn will come one day. We shall not exercise our office for ever. At most for a few short years will it be entrusted to us, and any day our ministry may end. But whether the time

be short or long, we must work on happily
and hopefully, ready to obey the call to stay
where we are, to go elsewhere—it may be
far hence to the heathen, or perhaps to higher
service above. For that I said our own turn
will come some day. That is true. But it
may not come through physical death. The
Lord may will that we tarry till He come,
and He may be coming quickly. Let us be
careful to work and watch with life—not
death—in view, "looking for that blessed hope,
and the glorious appearing of our great God
and our Saviour Jesus Christ" (Titus ii. 13).
We are often content with lower ideals, but
we must lift up our hearts unto the Lord, and
we must take Him at His word. "And
when the chief Shepherd shall appear, ye
shall receive a crown of glory that fadeth
not away" (1 St. Peter v. 4).

"Now the God of peace, that brought
again from the dead our Lord Jesus, that
Great Shepherd of the Sheep, through the
Blood of the everlasting covenant, make you
perfect in every good work to do His will,
working in you that which is well pleasing
in His sight; to Whom be glory for ever
and ever. Amen" (Hebrews xiii. 20, 21).

INDEX.

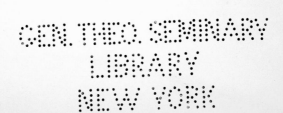

REFERENCES TO PASSAGES OF HOLY SCRIPTURE.

GLASGOW: PRINTED AT THE UNIVERSITY PRESS BY ROBERT MACLEHOSE AND CO. LTD.

Macmillan and Co.'s New Works

Memoir of Archbishop Temple. By Seven Friends. Edited by E. G. SANDFORD, Archdeacon of Exeter. With Photogravure and other Illustrations. 2 vols. 8vo.

Earlier Years. By Canon J. M. WILSON, Worcester.
Education Office. By H. J. ROBY.
Rugby. By F. E. KITCHENER.
Exeter. By the Ven. Archdeacon SANDFORD.

London. By the Ven. Archdeacon BEVAN.
The Primacy. By the Right Rev. the LORD BISHOP OF BRISTOL.
Canterbury. By the Ven. Archdeacon SPOONER.

Editor's Supplement.

A History of the Christian Church from the Reformation to the Present Time. By S. CHEETHAM, D.D., Archdeacon and Canon of Rochester. Crown 8vo.

A History of the English Church. Edited by Dean STEPHENS and the Rev. W. HUNT, D.Litt. In 8 Volumes. Crown 8vo.

Vol. VII. The Eighteenth Century. By the Rev. Canon OVERTON, D.D., and the Rev. F. RELTON.

The Philosophy of Religion. By Prof. HARALD HÖFFDING. Translated by Miss B. E. MEYER. 8vo.

Essays on some Theological Questions of the Day. By Members of the University of Cambridge. Edited by HENRY BARCLAY SWETE, D.D., Regius Professor of Divinity. 8vo.

LIST OF CONTRIBUTORS.

THE EDITOR.
Rev. W. CUNNINGHAM, D.D.
Rev. F. R. TENNANT, B.D.
Rev. A. CALDECOTT, D.D.
W. L. H. DUCKWORTH, M.A., M.D.
Rev. E. H. ASKWITH, D.D.
Rev. J. M. WILSON, D.D.
Rev. A. W. ROBINSON, D.D.

Rev. J. O. F. MURRAY, D.D.
Rev. W. E. BARNES, D.D.
Rev. F. H. CHASE, D.D., Bishop-Designate of Ely.
Rev. A. J. MASON, D.D.
Rev. F. J. FOAKES-JACKSON, B.D.
Rev. J. F. BETHUNE-BAKER, B.D
Rev. H. M. BUTLER, D.D.

Idola Theatri: An Explanation of the Fallacious Principles that have hindered the Progress of Philosophy in recent years, further illustrated by criticisms of some leading Oxford thinkers. By HENRY STURT, M.A., editor of *Personal Idealism*. 8vo.

LONDON : MACMILLAN AND CO., LIMITED.

Macmillan and Co.'s New Works

The Apocalypse of St. John. The Greek Text, with Introduction, Notes, and Indices. By H. B. SWETE, D.D., Regius Professor of Divinity at Cambridge. 8vo.

An Analysis of St. Paul's Epistles. By J. B. LIGHTFOOT, D.D., sometime Bishop of Durham. 8vo.

St. Paul's Epistle to the Ephesians. The Greek Text, with Introduction and Notes. By Bishop WESTCOTT. 8vo.

A General View of the History of the English Bible. By BROOKE FOSS WESTCOTT, D.D., formerly Bishop of Durham. A New Edition. Revised by W. ALDIS WRIGHT, Litt.D. 8vo.

Life of the Right Rev. Bishop Westcott. By his Son, the Rev. ARTHUR WESTCOTT. Abridged Edition. Ex. Crown 8vo.

Conversations with Christ. A Biographical Study. By the Author of *The Faith of a Christian.* Crown 8vo.

An Enquiry into the Evidential Value of Prophecy. Being the Hulsean Prize Essay for 1904. By Rev. E. A. EDGHILL, B.A., Scholar of King's College, Cambridge. Crown 8vo.

The Church of Christ, its Life and Work. An attempt to trace the Work of the Church in some of its Departments from the Earliest Times to the Present Day. Baird Lectures. By Very Rev. Professor A. H. CHARTERIS, D.D. Crown 8vo.

Greatheart. Some Talks with Him. By a Pilgrim. Crown 8vo. 3s. net.

The Pastoral Idea. Lectures in Pastoral Theology delivered at King's College, London, during the Lent Term, 1905. By Rev. J. T. INSKIP. Crown 8vo.

Jesus Christ and the Christian Character. By FRANCIS GREENWOOD PEABODY, Plummer Professor of Christian Morals in Harvard University, and author of *The Religion of an Educated Man, Jesus Christ and the Social Question,* etc. Crown 8vo.

LONDON : MACMILLAN AND CO., LIMITED.

2

Works by Bishop Westcott, D.D.

Words of Faith and Hope. Crown 8vo. 4s. 6d.

Lessons from Work. Crown 8vo. 6s.

A General Survey of the History of the Canon of the New Testament during the First Four Centuries. Sixth Edition. Crown 8vo. 10s. 6d.

The Bible in the Church: A Popular Account of the Collection and Reception of the Holy Scriptures in the Christian Churches. Tenth Edition. Pott 8vo. 4s. 6d.

Introduction to the Study of the Four Gospels. Eighth Edition. 10s. 6d.

The Gospel of the Resurrection. Thoughts on its Relation to Reason and History. Sixth Edition. Crown 8vo. 6s.

The Revelation of the Risen Lord. Fourth Edition. Crown 8vo. 6s.

The Historic Faith. Short Lectures on the Apostles' Creed. Third Edition. Crown 8vo. 6s.

The Revelation of the Father. Short Lectures on the Titles of the Lord in the Gospel of St. John. Second Edition. Crown 8vo. 6s.

Christus Consummator, and other Sermons. Crown 8vo. 6s.

Social Aspects of Christianity. Second Edition. Crown 8vo. 6s.

Gifts for Ministry. Addresses to Candidates for Ordinations. Crown 8vo. 1s. 6d.

The Epistle to the Hebrews. The Greek Text, with Notes and Essays. New Edition. 8vo. 14s.

The Epistles of St. John. The Greek Text, with Notes and Essays. Third Edition. 8vo. 12s. 6d.

The Incarnation and Common Life. Crown 8vo. 9s.

Christian Aspects of Life. Crown 8vo. 7s. 6d.

The Gospel of Life: Thoughts Introductory to the Study of Christian Doctrine. Crown 8vo. 6s.

Essays—The History of Religious Thought in the West. Globe 8vo. 4s. net. *[Eversley Series.*

On Some Points in the Religious Office of the Universities. Crown 8vo. 4s. 6d.

Some Thoughts from the Ordinal. Globe 8vo. 1s 6d.

Thoughts on Revelation and Life. Being Selections from the Writings of Bishop WESTCOTT. Arranged and Edited by Rev. STEPHEN PHILLIPS. Crown 8vo. 6s.

The Obligations of Empire. A Sermon. Crown 8vo. Sewed. 3d. net.

Christian Social Union Addresses. Crown 8vo. 1s. net.

Common Prayers for Family Use. Crown 8vo. 1s. net.

Peterborough Sermons. Crown 8vo. 6s.

Life of the Right Rev. Bishop Westcott. By his Son, the Rev. ARTHUR WESTCOTT. Two Vols. Extra Crown 8vo. 17s. net. Also 1 Vol. Abridged Edition. Ex. Crown 8vo.

By BISHOP WESTCOTT and Dr. F. J. A. HORT.

The New Testament in the Original Greek. 8vo. 10s. net.

The New Testament in the Original Greek. Vol. I., Text. Vol. II., Introduction and Appendix. Crown 8vo. 10s. 6d. each. Pott 8vo Edition, 4s. 6d.; Roan, 5s. 6d.; Morocco, 6s. 6d.; India Paper Edition, Limp Calf, 7s. 6d. net.

LONDON: MACMILLAN AND CO., LIMITED.

A HISTORY OF
THE ENGLISH CHURCH

EDITED BY THE LATE

VERY REV. W. R. W. STEPHENS, D.D.

DEAN OF WINCHESTER

AND

THE REV. WILLIAM HUNT, LITT.D.

A Continuous History, based upon a careful Study of Original
Authorities, and of the best Ancient and Modern Writers.

In Eight Volumes, uniform binding, Crown 8vo.   With Maps.

Each Vol. is sold separately, and has its own Index.

Vol.   I.—**The English Church from its Foundation to the Norman
Conquest.** By the Rev. WILLIAM HUNT, Litt.D.
7s. 6d.   [*Ready.*

Vol.   II.—**The English Church from the Norman Conquest to
the Accession of Edward I.** By DEAN STEPHENS.
7s. 6d.   [*Ready.*

Vol.   III.—**The English Church in the Fourteenth and Fifteenth
Centuries.** By the Rev. Canon CAPES, late Fellow of
Queen's College, Oxford. 7s. 6d.   [*Ready.*

Vol.   IV.—**The English Church in the Sixteenth Century from
the Accession of Henry VIII. to the Death of Mary.**
By JAMES GAIRDNER, Esq., C.B., LL.D. 7s. 6d.
[*Ready.*

Vol.   V.—**The English Church in the Reigns of Elizabeth and
James I.** By the Rev. W. H. FRERE. 7s. 6d. [*Ready.*

Vol.   VI.—**The English Church from the Accession of Charles I.
to the Death of Anne.** By the Rev. W. H. HUTTON,
B.D., Fellow of St. John's College, Oxford. 7s. 6d.
[*Ready.*

Vol.   VII.—**The English Church in the Eighteenth Century.** By
the Rev. Canon OVERTON, D.D., and the Rev. F.
RELTON. 7s. 6d.

Vol.   VIII.—**The English Church in the Nineteenth Century.** By
F. WARRE CORNISH, M.A., Vice-Provost of Eton
College.   [*In preparation.*

LONDON ; MACMILLAN AND CO., LIMITED.

4